CONTENTS
AEROPLANE YEARBOOK 2023-24

32

14

AEROPLANE YEARBOOK 2023-24

ISBN 978-1-80282-852-8

Editor: Ben Dunnell
Senior editor, specials: Roger Mortimer
E-mail: roger.mortimer@keypublishing.com
Design: Craig Chiswell
Advertising Sales Manager: Brodie Baxter
E-mail: brodie.baxter@keypublishing.com
Tel: 01780 755131
Advertising Production: Debi McGowan
E-mail: debi.mcgowan@keypublishing.com

SUBSCRIPTION/MAIL ORDER
Key Publishing Ltd, PO Box 300,
Stamford, Lincs, PE9 1NA
Tel: 01780 480404
Subscriptions e-mail:
subs@keypublishing.com
Mail Order e-mail:
orders@keypublishing.com
Website: www.keypublishing.com/shop

PUBLISHING
Group CEO: Adrian Cox
Published by: Key Publishing Ltd, PO Box
100, Stamford, Lincs, PE9 1XQ
Tel: 01780 755131
Website: www.keypublishing.com

PRINTING
Precision Colour Printing Ltd, Haldane,
Halesfield 1, Telford, Shropshire. TF7 4QQ

DISTRIBUTION
Seymour Distribution Ltd, 2 Poultry
Avenue, London, EC1A 9PU
Enquiries Line: 020 7429 4000

Cover image:
No 74 Squadron Lightning F1s on a sortie from Coltishall in 1961.
AEROPLANE, COLOURISED BY RICHARD JAMES MOLLOY

90

Surely the highlight of any historic airshow in 2023: the Me 262 A/B-1c from the Messerschmitt Stiftung leads Mistral Warbirds' Canadair Sabre Mk6 and the Fundacja Eskadra's Lim-2 in a formation flypast of swept-wing jets, mounted uniquely by the Air Legend event at Melun-Villaroche, France, in September. BEN DUNNELL

CONNECT WITH US!

 www.facebook.com/AeroplaneMonthly
 @HistoryInTheAir

www. **KEY.AERO**

WELCOME

AEROPLANE YEARBOOK 2023-24

The whole team behind *Aeroplane* is delighted to bring you our *Yearbook 2023-2024*, featuring some of our best features from the year gone by and some exclusive, new reading. What a year it's been, not least as we celebrated the 50th anniversary of this monthly magazine. You'll find insights into some of aviation history's most enthralling subjects, ranging from the light aeroplane pioneers who lined up at Lympne a century ago to inside stories of such great Cold War warriors as the U-2, the Lightning and the Victor. And we bring you up to date with the preservation scene, including the very latest news on the return to airworthiness of a special Spitfire, the delightful restoration of a classic British airliner, and fresh detail about a fascinating Messerschmitt Bf 109 E project. Such are the great articles *Aeroplane* showcases every month — and 2024 promises to bring you many more of them.

Ben Dunnell, *editor*

PRESERVATION REVIEW OF 2023

Chronicling an extremely busy year in the aviation heritage world **WORDS:** BEN DUNNELL

The highlights tell their own story. A Hawker Tempest flying for the first time in decades, several other very important restorations reaching completion on different continents — the airworthy historic aircraft scene continues to show no signs of slowing down. Nor was there any shortage of activity among museums large and small, even if the current trend for airframes among the major UK institutions favours departures over arrivals. Surely the archaeological story of the year is the Messerschmitt Bf 109 F wreck find in Malta, led by members of the Malta Aviation Museum, the like of which is the stuff of dreams. Certain threats did rear their head: the fate of the Cornwall Aviation Heritage Centre shows how an attraction's tenure can be ended with the proverbial stroke of a pen, while Switzerland's airworthy classic jet fleet has gone from Europe's strongest to almost non-existent. But read our 2023 preservation chronology, and you realise the year has brought us more than it's taken away.

Pete Kynsey brings Fighter Aviation Engineering's Tempest II in to land at Duxford, at the conclusion of its maiden post-restoration flight. TONY CLARKE

JANUARY

9 Sole surviving Waco UOC Custom, ZK-AEL, flies for the first time in nearly 65 years at Omaka, New Zealand

13 The rear fuselage of the South Yorkshire Aircraft Museum's Lancaster X, KB976, is mated with the fuselage of NX611 at the Lincolnshire Aviation Heritage Centre to allow the latter to continue taxi runs during its restoration to airworthiness

FEBRUARY

6 The Spitfire Company and flyaspitfire.com announce that they have commissioned an airworthy Mosquito FBVI restoration from Avspecs at Ardmore, New Zealand, and that the aircraft will arrive at Biggin Hill during 2026

10 Having been sold by the Fly Navy Heritage Trust, ex-Fleet Air Arm Phantom FG1 XV586 leaves RNAS Yeovilton, bound for the Morayvia museum at Kinloss

21 At Wangaratta, New South Wales, P-40N Kittyhawk NZ3184/VH-EPU — a wartime Royal New Zealand Air Force combat veteran — completes its maiden flight after restoration

23 The first flight of Charles Somers' DH89B Dominie, ZK-AKU (to become NX663HG), on completion by Avspecs of its restoration at Ardmore

MARCH

6 Excavation begins of an incredible discovery in Malta, found during building work at a care home: the substantial remains of a Messerschmitt Bf 109 F-4, Werknummer 8668, shot down by anti-aircraft fire on 1 April 1942

24 The latest RAF Museum disposal is announced, as Stow Maries Great War Aerodrome in Essex buys its Sopwith Tabloid replica

27 Owned by Fighter Aviation Engineering and restored by Air Leasing at Sywell, the ex-Sidney Cotton pre-war photo-reconnaissance Lockheed 12A, G-AFTL, flies for the first time in Britain since 1940; it subsequently takes up residence at Duxford

27 Built by Achim Engels in Germany and finished off in New Zealand, the Vintage Aviator's Fokker E.III reproduction ZK-EIN takes to the air at Masterton

30 The IWM's TBM-3E Avenger leaves Duxford; initially stored outside at the Wirral Transport Museum and Heritage Tramway in Birkenhead, it will go on show in a future Battle of the Atlantic museum in the Merseyside town

APRIL

1 As the Kent Battle of Britain Museum at Hawkinge reopens for the summer season, ex-RAF Museum CASA 352L T.2B-272 goes on show at its new home, refinished as a Luftwaffe Ju 52/3m

4 Cornwall Council formally requests clearance of the Newquay Airport site occupied by the Cornwall Aviation Heritage Centre, ending its chances of reopening and forcing new homes to be found for its aircraft

6 Disposed of by the RAF Museum, P-51D Mustang 44-73415 arrives with its new owner, the Hunter Fighter Collection at Scone, New South Wales

7 Spitfire IX TE517, owned by 517 Ltd, flies after being put back into the air by the Biggin Hill-based Spitfire Company

14 Official opening of the Amelia Earhart Hangar Museum at the airport bearing her name in Atchison, Kansas

22 The oldest surviving BN-2 Islander, G-AVCN, is unveiled at the Wight Military and Heritage Museum on the Isle of Wight; it had been restored by the Britten-Norman Aircraft Preservation Society

23 Slingsby-built SE5a film replica G-AVOU flies again at Sywell, with restorer Matthew Boddington at the helm

MAY

2 Road-transported from Austria, Vickers Viking G-AGRW arrives at Blackbushe for restoration and preservation by the Blackbushe Heritage Trust

12 A three-year Airbus sponsorship deal is announced by The People's Mosquito for its airworthy Mosquito FBVI build project

15 Restored by AirCorps Aviation at Bemidji, Minnesota, the Dakota Territory Air Museum's P-47D Thunderbolt 42-27609 flies again

25 In a difficult year for Swiss classic jet operations, which also sees the country's last flyable two-seat Hunter being sold, the Espace Passion association's Mirage IIIDS J-2012/HB-RDF makes its final flight before an enforced, permanent grounding

27 At Everett, Washington, the Flying Heritage and Combat Armor Museum reopens after three years of closure, now under the ownership of Steuart Walton

16 The RAF Museum opens new Bomber Command exhibitions at both its London (Hendon) and Midlands (Cosford) sites; sections of Stirling III LK488 are displayed at both, having been stored for years, while newly restored Wellington X MF628 is the centrepiece at Cosford

JUNE

6 Another restoration by AirCorps Aviation, P-51C Mustang racer N5528N *Thunderbird*, makes its maiden flight — in natural metal at this stage

14 In advance of a spectacular Italian Air Force centenary show at Pratica di Mare, Renzo Catellani's Fiat G91R/1A MM6305/I-AMIC flies after restoration at Piacenza

16 Reopening of the Italian Air Force Museum at Vigna di Valle, an 18-month refurbishment having been completed

19 Work on the aircraft finished by Dirk Bende and his team, Eberhard Thiesen's Messerschmitt Bf 109 E-4, Werknummer 1983/D-FEML, performs its first post-restoration flight at Bonn-Hangelar, Germany with Charlie Brown at the controls

27 Sea Venom FAW21 WM571 moves from the Bournemouth Aviation Museum to the Classic British Jet Collection at Bruntingthorpe, where it will be restored to running condition

21 Lockheed C-121A 48-613/N422NA, owned by Lewis Air Legends — and best-known in USAF service as Gen Douglas MacArthur's staff transport, named *Bataan* — flies following restoration by Fighter Rebuilders at Chino

JULY

10 Repatriated from South Africa, Lightning F6 XP693 arrives in a container at the former RAF Binbrook, Lincolnshire — a 91st birthday gift to ex-Lightning pilot AVM George Black

15 The Military Aviation Museum at Virginia Beach receives C-46F Commando 44-78774/N78774 *Tinker Belle*

15-16 Ending an absence from the calendar since 2019, The Fighter Collection's Flying Legends Air Show is revived at Leeds East Airport, Yorkshire — the former RAF Church Fenton

28 Brokered by Boschung Global, the sale is announced of the Hangar 10 fleet of warbirds at Heringsdorf, Germany; its purchaser is another German collector, Karl Grimminger

AUGUST

4 Navy Wings appeals for ex-Fairey Gannet mechanics to assist with a plan to return Gannet T5 XT752 to the air and bring it back to the UK

6 The Yorkshire Air Museum at Elvington receives Jaguar GR1 XZ383 from Cosford, where it had been an instructional airframe

8 Raytheon's veteran Convair CV-580 testbed N580HH is retired to the Pima Air and Space Museum in Arizona

9 The Intrepid Air, Sea and Space Museum's Concorde, G-BOAD, travels down the Hudson River for refurbishment at the Brooklyn Navy Yard

13 Both crew members escape successfully as Dan Filer's ex-Czech Air Force MiG-23UB, 8107/N23UB, crashes in Belleville, Michigan during the Thunder over Michigan airshow at nearby Willow Run; nor are there any injuries on the ground

17 IWM Duxford takes Firefly I Z2033 back from loan to the Fleet Air Arm Museum after 23 years

24 Another Jaguar leaves Cosford: 'raspberry ripple' ex-Empire Test Pilots' School T2 XX145, bound for the Boscombe Down Aviation Collection at Old Sarum

25 P-51D Mustang 45-11518/ G-CLNV, restored by Air Leasing as a two-seat TF-51D, flies at Sywell; soon afterwards it's delivered to its new owner, the W Aircollection at La Ferté-Alais, France

SEPTEMBER

26 The National Museum of the US Air Force announces the latest addition to its collection: an ex-Ukrainian Air Force two-seat Sukhoi Su-27UB, '32 blue', which arrived in the US during 2009 and had been on the civil register as N132SU

6 Newly acquired by Swiss owner Hugo Mathys, B-25D Mitchell 43-3318/ N88972 completes a ferry flight from Spokane — its former home with the Historic Flight Foundation — to Madras, Washington, where it will be prepared for a trans-Atlantic flight

8 The Collings Foundation announces the acquisition of P-47D Thunderbolt 45-49167 from the National Museum of the US Air Force, in exchange for a PT-17 Kaydet; the 'Jug' will be surveyed to see if an airworthy restoration is possible

17 The last edition of the National Championship Air Races to be staged at Reno, Nevada, comes to a sad and premature conclusion when a collision after the T-6 Gold race kills first and second-placed pilots Chris Rushing and Nick Macy

19 Westland Wallace II K6035 returns to the RAF Museum London from storage, in advance of a new inter-war exhibition

29 P-3K2 Orion NZ4203 arrives with the Air Force Museum of New Zealand at Wigram, following a 280-mile road journey from RNZAF Base Woodbourne

OCTOBER

9 British owner David Nock's P-51D Mustang 44-84952/N210D makes its maiden post-restoration flight at Danville, Illinois, having been returned to flight by Midwest Aero Restorations

10 A tremendous milestone for the UK warbird scene, as Fighter Aviation Engineering's Tempest II MW763/G-TEMT flies from Sywell following restoration by Air Leasing — it becomes the first example of the Hawker fighter to take to the air for somewhere in the region of 70 years

10 At Nîmes-Alès-Camargue-Cévennes Airport in France, ex-Sécurité Civile Conair Turbo Firecat code T15 — under test

registration F-WYFT — makes its initial flight as an historic aircraft, owned by the Amicale Alençonnaise des Avions Anciens

17 One of the great pioneers of New Zealand's warbird movement, Wanaka-based Alpine Fighter Collection founder Sir Tim Wallis, dies aged 85

21 An appeal is launched to raise funds for the move of Sea Vixen XP924 from Yeovilton to the Bournemouth Aviation Museum, which has acquired it from Navy Wings

24 The RAF Museum's two-seat Focke-Wulf Fw 190 F-8/U1 Werknummer 584219 — a unique survivor of the

variant — leaves Hendon on loan to the Militärhistorisches Museum der Bundeswehr at Berlin-Gatow

NOVEMBER

2 A statement from the Newark Air Museum confirms it will not be receiving Eurofighter Typhoon DA4 (ZH590), which was expected to arrive from IWM Duxford; instead it will leave for Cosford, to become an instructional airframe

SUBSCRIBE

FlyPast is internationally regarded as the magazine for aviation history and heritage.

shop.keypublishing.com/fpsubs

Britain at War is dedicated to exploring every aspect of the involvement of Britain and her Commonwealth in conflicts from the turn of the 20th century through to the present day.

shop.keypublishing.com/bawsubs

ORDER DIRECT FROM OUR SHOP...
shop.keypublishi

OR CALL +44 (0)1780 480404
(Lines open 9.00-5.30, Monday-Friday GMT)

859/23

TODAY

Aeroplane is still providing the best aviation coverage around. With focus on iconic military aircraft from the 1930s to the 1960s.

shop.keypublishing.com/amsubs

Aviation News is renowned for providing the best coverage of every branch of aviation.

shop.keypublishing.com/ansubs

ng.com

PICTURE PERFECT

A primary aim in restoring Spitfire PRIV AA810 to flying condition is to pay tribute to the RAF's photo-reconnaissance squadrons — and, what's more, to do so with an utterly meticulous rebuild of this very rare machine

WORDS: BEN DUNNELL

Alastair 'Sandy' Gunn leaning on the tail of Spitfire R7056 in November 1941. GUNN FAMILY

The only known photo of Spitfire PRIV AA810 in service shows Flt Sgt Robert Tomlinson taxiing the aeroplane at Wick on 29 January 1942, the day on which he flew it to Trondheim and photographed the _Tirpitz_. TOMLINSON FAMILY

t may not look very much to the uninitiated eye, but the signs are there. A wide-open expanse in the Oxfordshire countryside, just north-west of the village of Berinsfield — just another piece of farmland, one might think. But the tell-tale areas of disused concrete help give it away, and on closer examination with the benefit of local knowledge, its airfield origins are rendered clear. This is the former RAF Mount Farm, one-time satellite to nearby Benson, subsequently known in its own right as US Army Air Forces Station 234. The latter period is marked not far away by a memorial incorporating a mock-up Supermarine Spitfire propeller, in honour of the 7th Photographic Group. But of activities here by the RAF's No 1 Photographic Reconnaissance Unit, there is rather less recognition. A current — indeed, a unique — restoration project aims to change that.

Two stories are being brought together, of man and machine. Flt Lt Alastair 'Sandy' Gunn had been flying the Avro Ansons of No 48 Squadron on coastal patrols out of Stornoway when he was recommended for a posting to the Photographic Reconnaissance Unit, as No 1 PRU was then still known. Having arrived at Benson, the PRU's base, his first Spitfire flight came on 8 September 1941. Initially the young man from Auchterarder, Perthshire, found its speed hard to cope with and landings a particular challenge. But 'circuits and bumps' at Mount Farm, which had proper runways, helped him improve. Rapidly he felt much more confident. All Gunn's further training was done from Mount Farm, returning to Benson at each day's end.

With only 11 flights on type — all on Spitfire PRI models at this stage — 'Sandy' was declared operational, being assigned to 'D' Flight. His maiden sortie took him from Benson to Le Havre on 16 September. Soon the longer-range PRIV was available, with additional fuel tankage and the more powerful Rolls-Royce Merlin 45 engine. One such was AA810, built at different garage complexes in Reading to which production had been dispersed, with final assembly taking place in a Vickers-Supermarine facility established at RAF Henley. AA810 left Henley on 19 October 1941. It went to Benson to be fitted-out with cameras, and then a few days later to Mount Farm, where it was based with 'C' Flight,

No 1 PRU. There the author found himself standing on the remains of one of the runways with AA810's owner Tony Hoskins, the man behind its resurrection.

All the aircraft's missions were mounted from the satellite airfield, until 'C' Flight moved to Wick in the far north-east of Scotland during January 1942. Having dropped off his two-litre Lagonda at Benson, Gunn borrowed a 'B' Flight aeroplane for his transit north on the 21st, making it to Leuchars where he

> ## 66 *AA810 was hit in the starboard-wing fuel tank and caught fire* 99

made a flapless, brakeless landing. The flight's task was to search for the German battleship *Tirpitz*, which 'C' Flight pilot Flt Lt A. F. P. Fane photographed in Trondheim harbour during his 23 January sortie. 'Sandy' was kept at Leuchars for the time being, allowing operations to be mounted from there if the Wick weather was out of limits. He finally rejoined his five colleagues on 5 February.

Several times the No 1 PRU Spitfires captured important images of *Tirpitz* over the weeks that

followed, Gunn doing so for the first time on 19 February at the controls of AA797. In his diary, entries from which are reproduced in Tony Hoskins' book *Sandy's Spitfire* (Independent Publishing Network, 2019), he described the spectacle of the battleship under way as "a magnificent sight with the green water, bright sun, white smoke and brown wake."

He was earmarked for his first mission in AA810 on 5 March, again heading to Trondheim. But this time the Germans, helped by improved listening facilities near Kristiansand, were waiting. Two Messerschmitt Bf 109s assigned to Jagdgeschwader 1 at Lade were scrambled after the incoming PR aircraft. As it happened, Gunn had decided to turn back for home with a rough-running engine. In clear weather and generating light condensation, his Spitfire was easy to see. In his unarmed machine, 'Sandy' sought to out-run his pursuers, but AA810 was hit in the starboard-wing fuel tank and caught fire. He had no option but to bail out, coming down in the area of Surnadal. The Spitfire crashed nearby, bringing an end to its 16th operational sortie.

Met and assisted initially by Norwegian locals, Gunn recognised that his chances of evading capture were all but non-existent. He duly handed himself in to German forces and was taken prisoner, eventually being transported to Stalag Luft III near what was then Sagan, Lower ➲

Silesia. There on the night of 24-25 March 1944 he was among the 76 Allied servicemen involved in the 'Great Escape', but in 'Sandy's' case recapture came soon after, some 25 miles from Stettin. Interrogated at Görlitz, he and his fellow escapees gave nothing away. 'Sandy' was executed on 6 April, his ashes today resting in Poznan Old Garrison Cemetery.

Walking along one of Mount Farm's derelict runways, Tony Hoskins points out what appears to be a pile of assorted junk, but includes discarded sections of a former PSP (pierced steel planking) landing strip, and possibly some other significant relics in broken-down form. Not far away, an original wartime windsock post still stands. "We want to bring '810 back here when it's flown", says Tony, a long-time aircraft engineer — not least for existing warbird operators — who was instrumental in recovering the airframe. He's looking towards 2025, and a period of crop rotation, to facilitate provision of a temporary strip at Mount Farm and the Spitfire's ability to land on.

Before that, though, there's a restoration to finish. It was in the summer of 2018, following a tip-off, that a team led by Tony Hoskins recovered AA810's wreckage from Surnadal. "We found about 75 per cent of the aircraft", he says. "The tail had broken off on the descent — later research we did through 2020 found that the tail had fallen in the fjord 'next door', where it remained until about 15 years ago and then was scrapped."

What remained was brought to the UK, and rapidly entered restoration. "There were a number of things we wanted to do with the wreck before we pulled it apart to recover parts from it", recalls Tony, "so we decided to go for a completely brand new-build tail unit to start with. We kicked off with that on the anniversary of the shoot-down of the aeroplane, so on 5 March, but this time in 2019 — 77 years after it was shot down — we started the build with a fin and a set of tailplanes. That was helped

> **❝ Under the CAA, we have to justify everything as to what is a PRIV ❞**

very generously by somebody who wanted to see the project get going, and we could run that in the background while we launched the youth scheme and everything else. It wasn't until early October 2019 that we moved all of the wreck to the Isle of Wight for parts recovery. We instructed Airframe Assemblies to strip the entire fuselage.

"We have been hugely fortunate to have worked with some fantastic companies and individuals through the last few years. Times have been tough for everybody, but by running the project efficiently and using the funds we have effectively, we've managed to really move this restoration along. The team, both around me and those we contract across the UK, all want to see 'Sandy's' Spitfire fly, and at the same time be the most accurate restoration we can achieve. We started with a very busy 2019 and we were gathering lots of parts, because I want to use as many original systems and components as possible. I was also acquiring other wreckage which had salvageable bits on it. COVID really hit us hard, but we managed to keep progress steady throughout to the point that we are in a fantastic position now.

"The issue with the PRIV is that it is a converted MkI. AA810 started as part of the second order of 500 MkIs, ordered in July 1940, so it was destined to be a fighter. It was also built in a dispersed factory. We were finding things that were built to different patterns, different dates, different mod states. Indeed, recent research work from pulling apart the wreckage shows that AA810 had a fuselage already completed in a fighter configuration — all the modifications for reconnaissance work have been added afterwards! Of course, under the CAA, we have to justify everything as to what is a PRIV. I found the PRIV modification book in Kew [at the National Archives], so I thought, 'Great, that's going to tell me all the mod states between a MkI and a PRIV'. It didn't at all. Again, I was back to square one of going through literally every single bit of wreckage. We stored all of the wings in a shipping container on the Isle of Wight, and I would go down there every couple of months and sit there for hours on end going through every little bit: 'That's a MkI part, that's a specific PRIV part, that's a MkII part' and so on, seeing if we could reference them to the drawings so we knew where we were going with things.

"Then COVID hit. To maintain safe and steady progress we effectively broke the whole aeroplane down into 'kits', and I worked it all out — the rear fuselage kit is going to cost me this, the forward fuselage kit is going to cost me this, the main structural bits that we have to replace anyway because they're too corroded are going to cost me this — to see what I could space out over the next six months so we still could continue with progress, but not tying

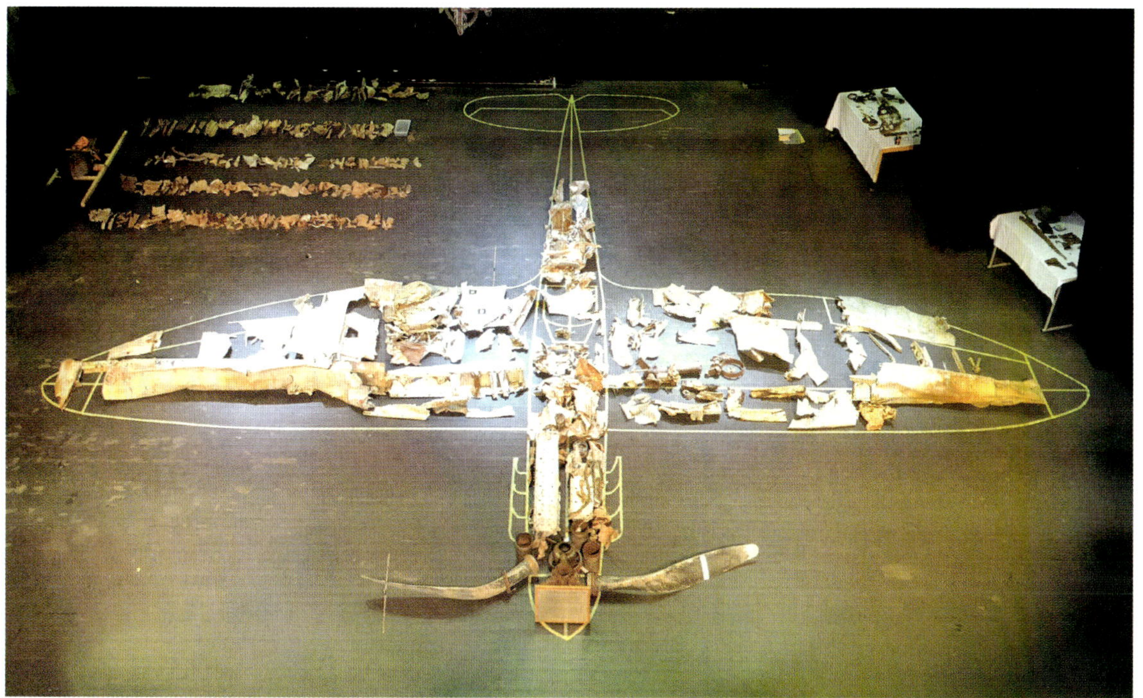

LEFT:
The remains of AA810 laid out in Surnadal following their recovery. It was deduced from the wreck that the engine had stopped at the time of impact, and that the combat encounter with the two Bf 109s had riddled the Spitfire with nearly 200 bullet holes. TONY HOSKINS

ourselves up so much financially that if the world fell over, I'd end up owing lots of money.

❖

"At the same time, I could buy systems bits and pieces from people clearing out their collections for COVID-related reasons. I started to get all the instrumentation, the cameras, camera mounts and little fittings that are unique to the project.

I could also do a huge amount of research, because research is free. I gathered photos of camera installations and so on, because then I could feed all that into the system, and do that hard work for Airframe Assemblies. In advance of making something, all the drawings, all the information and all the references would be there, so we could write the AAN [airworthiness approval note] for the CAA as we go, saying, 'A PRIV is a MkI with this, this and this.' I spent an awful lot of 2020 doing that.

"Research really is the key to getting a restoration right, particularly when you are restoring a type not seen before. When first going through the wreck there are so many unknowns — often, items would carry a part number, but if the drawing didn't exist while it was possible to assign it to an area or a system, its purpose or indeed its actual shape was still near-impossible to fathom. As time has gone on and we have learned more and more, there are items we are finally identifying today that we have been unsure about for coming up to five years! It really is a fascinating experience.

"Getting into the early part of 2021, I'd been trying to reach out to businesses quite a lot. One of the ways we try to involve young people in this, and companies in particular, is that we obviously need some money to build the aeroplane, we need materials to build the aeroplane, and we need labour and services to build the aeroplane. Machining costs are getting more and more expensive, pattern-making is getting more and more expensive, and ultimately the money is used to pay for labour. If we can reduce labour costs as much as we can, that's great, but you want the right labour.

"I started reaching out all the way through COVID to aerospace companies and their apprenticeship schemes… we were in a bit of a ➲

LEFT:
The completed fin unit for AA810 in May 2020. TONY HOSKINS

ABOVE:
With two cameras mounted vertically, the control cables for elevator and rudder control have to be diverted around the lens. Here the control diverter beam is fitted into the lower longerons in the immediate foreground.
AIRFRAME ASSEMBLIES

RIGHT:
The collection of camera equipment being stripped and painstakingly worked on by Thales apprentices to return three cameras to service at the firm's Glasgow site.
SPITFIRE AA810

unarmed example helps. "Also, photo-reconnaissance very much relates to today's ISTAR [intelligence, surveillance, target acquisition and reconnaissance], and 'eyes in the sky'. The future of where the air force is going largely is UAVs, 'swarm' drones and that sort of thing — the same roles the reconnaissance guys did during the war.

"One of the things I did during COVID was I sat down with the Supermarine suppliers list, which I think was 317 different companies, and traced every single company — where they'd gone, who they'd been bought out by, whether they were still in existence. In some cases, they've gone into their archives and still got original examples of stock they made in the war that's never been issued, and that we managed to get bits and pieces from. Every lead is worth following. Some have paid off, some have not, but it meant I managed to get down to a list of 17-18 different companies in existence today that are either still in the business, in a financial position to help, or are in a position where they need to bring in younger staff. I was able to offer them something through the youth scheme that ticks all their boxes, in exchange for access to their facilities or use of their existing apprenticeship programme to do this."

As Tony points out, for younger people well-versed in the latest technology, a Spitfire isn't the most difficult task they'll be faced with. "At the time, it was very complex compared to a Hurricane. Relative to today, it's massively over-engineered in various ways, but easy if you've got a five-axis CNC [computer numerical control] machine.

"By doing that far enough in advance, I was getting items made through 2021-22 that I don't need until now. It puts low pressure on the company, because they fit it in. The apprentices learn from it, they get assessed on it, we give them all the support they need as part of their assessments, and it doesn't cost me anything. That way, I can massively progress the background work on things, so now we have started wing assembly, I've got a nice, big box of stuff that's all been calculated and anodised and NDT'ed [subjected to non-destructive testing] and everything else that's ready to go. That means we can bring it together more efficiently, requiring less time in the jig. Paying for less time in the jig means the money I've got goes further in progressing this."

A very good example of a leading industry name that's become heavily engaged in AA810's restoration is GKN Aerospace. One of the UK's foremost global suppliers in the field, GKN has had considerable direct involvement since early 2022. There's an historical link here too, for during World War Two the GKN plant at

> ## " *Paying for less time in the jig means the funds go further* "

stalemate. We'd worked a lot on the charitable aspect, but effectively, other than buying parts, we hadn't progressed the restoration significantly for five or six months. Then the 2021 spring budget came out, and a number of the companies I'd been talking to were able to look at the project. It has boomed from there.

"But you obviously have to work through lots of these things. So, while I'd brought undercarriage legs and was asking companies to overhaul them, they'd say yes, but I'd have to go and find the documentation. I had a frustrating time in that I had all these agreements in place with companies who wanted to do the work, but I had to find the information. Of course, so much of it was withheld by other companies, and I had to start going to meetings with them. A lot of 2021 was spent getting all of this aligned. Suddenly it all kicked off, and companies were saying, 'Bring it all in — we'll do it'. Since then, my feet haven't touched the ground."

Why has AA810's rebuild generated such corporate interest? "It's got a nice story", says Tony, adding that the fact of it being an

Hadley Castle near Telford — known for its manufacturing of wheels — produced in excess of 1,000 Spitfire fuselages, which then went to the Vickers-Supermarine 'shadow factory' in Castle Bromwich for final assembly. What's more, GKN's East Cowes, Isle of Wight facility turned out Spitfire parts, among them fuselage frame and systems components for AA810 itself. That very factory is just seven miles from the Sandown premises of Airframe Assemblies, where the restoration is progressing. And it's now playing its own role.

❖

"They're doing it over a large number of sites", reports Tony. "GKN in Bristol is currently machining up all the wing machine fittings we need for the spar, a lot of the rib feet that go on the back of the spar, aileron fittings and that sort of thing. GKN in Luton is doing the photo-reconnaissance blisters that go on the side of the canopy. I managed to find one drawing, which came from a lorry driver who was delivering some parts. He went, 'Oh, I've got a load of Spitfire drawings'. He brought them over on his next delivery trip, and he had the blisters. It was unbelievable. There were only general arrangement drawings in the PRIV notes, but this was an actual dimensions drawing with the thicknesses and everything else. We've given those to GKN Luton and they're now making the tooling for the blisters.

"All the heat treatments on main spars were having to be done in Coventry. You had to take main spars, which are fairly delicate, put them on a lorry, transport them, get them heat-treated and bring them back, running the risk of damage and everything else. GKN has ovens on the Isle of Wight, so as part of this we've managed to say that the heat treatment process is special and the apprentices can learn from that. We now get them done on the Isle of Wight. They can be taken down, done that afternoon and picked up the next day!

"At the same time, GKN on the Isle of Wight specialises in fuel tanks. The PRIV had a very special fuel system, and Airframe Assemblies has created a sheet metal kit for the fuel tanks which are now with GKN for assembly. They'll do the wet lay-ups, pressure-test them and everything else. I'm having tanks made six or seven months before I need

Pupils from Colfe's School in Greenwich with the 'travelling' Merlin engine belonging to the project's youth outreach programme. COLFE'S SCHOOL

A LONG LEGACY

There is a clear engineering connection to Spitfire AA810, not least through 'Sandy' Gunn himself, who did an apprenticeship at the Harland and Wolff shipyards in Glasgow before studying mechanical sciences at Pembroke College, Cambridge. An engineering outreach programme is, therefore, an obvious extension of the project, with the particular aim of encouraging into the aerospace industry members of new generations who may never have considered it before.

The project embarked upon its STEM outreach programme in September 2019. Educational resources have been put together with the help of experts and schools themselves. Now, just under 500 schools across the whole of the UK are being provided directly with free-of-charge careers advice, while a recently established partnership with Speakers for Schools takes in a further 2,000 state schools. Other activities include the likes of pilot inspiration days at active airfields, taking in hangar visits and simulator trips.

Of course, it's mutually beneficial. The broad aim is for industry to reap the future rewards of a newly engaged audience, but there's also the potential for a specific boost to the preservation scene. Involvement with AA810 on the part of companies which have not previously taken part in a restoration project, drawn in by the educational element, can see them using the latest technology for this purpose, such as 3D printing. This in turn may create new commercial opportunities. In October 2023, the project recorded its millionth engagement with a young person of school age — a milestone in itself.

TOP: Bicester-based Vintage Aircraft Radiators has tackled the radiator destined for AA810. That used on the aircraft was a Morris-pattern QCV-type, though it could have been made by one of several companies rather than Morris in Oxford itself. VIA TONY HOSKINS

MIDDLE: The top fuel tank internals — a complicated array of baffles and formers. With AA810's fuel tank having been ruptured and burnt, a new-made item will now be assembled by GKN apprentices. AIRFRAME ASSEMBLIES

ABOVE: The camera ports from the lower fuselage indicate how the whole lower fuselage, as found, was badly crushed. TONY HOSKINS

them, so that by the time the shell of the fuselage is done, I've got all the systems either overhauled, on a shelf or in the process of being done.

"We recovered about 200 parts from the lower fuselage, which are going back into the wreck. The wings — well, we have an awful lot of wing material. A lot of the aileron structure's going in, which is absolutely incredible because they looked really bad. When we pulled them apart, they weren't even corroded on the inside. There's as much original structure as possible going in, and with what doesn't go in the next priority is original wartime-manufactured parts. I've been buying other wrecks of other Spitfires, but I don't want anything in there from after [AA810] crashed other than new-build. If there's original wartime stuff, it's got to be pre-1941. Those parts either get patterned or used as swaps.

"Some things that have eluded me for a long time are trim units — I managed to get an original rudder trim unit the other day, and I'm trying to borrow an elevator trim now to see exactly how much it differs in body, because I'm going to have to make a new one. We're now getting to that position where, whilst I've found as much as I can, there comes a point where I'm just going to have to admit I need to make new. Another is the radiator door controls. I've got two crashed units which are not even worth recovering and are barely suitable as patterns, but I don't think I'm going to find another one, so I've just started the process now of getting them reverse-engineered. Again, we're trying to use apprentices for this. We've passed them back through the Airframe Assemblies QA [quality assurance] system to make approved drawings, and then we put them out for manufacture, sometimes again with our sponsoring companies who have the machine time to get it done.

"This year has been particularly good, as the fuselage is now almost completed. Using all our bench-prepared items from the last year of restoration has enabled the final fuselage assembly to progress really quickly. She is very recognisable as a Spitfire once more.

"The fin is completed, and the last of the machine fittings for the tailplane have now arrived. We're just awaiting some manpower slots for the tailplane; a lot of that we assembled in 2019 but couldn't finally assemble. I'm working at the moment on the engine mounts, trying to procure the right tube for the engine-bearers. We've done a huge amount on the component parts for the wings, from main spars to webs, leading-edge skins, rear spars, flap fittings, aileron fittings — there are so many parts on those wings it boggles the mind.

"Right now I'm expecting the fuselage out by Christmas, and the wings have just started. We're working hard on the system components with many items for the fuselage already overhauled, and others in work. Some have proved more of a challenge than we expected, but we are finding solutions to these.

"I took all the PR cameras to Thales in Glasgow last year, and

> **66** *I'm still confident we'll be airborne in May 2025* **99**

what a successful partnership that has been. Thales was born out of Vinten, and Vinten manufactured Williamson's wartime cameras. Their apprentices are putting together working cameras for us, so we'll have a full set of reconnaissance equipment in the machine. Very recently the first camera worked exactly as planned with all the original camera system controlling it. Now it just needs to take a photograph!

"But it's not without problems. We have issues over the de Havilland propeller, and the engine. Unfortunately, the engine we originally found is not as good as we thought it was, and it's presenting some challenges. We've been looking for a second engine for a long time as a spare, and we have a couple of options... Then there's the propeller, which is very particular to the early Spitfires. There are very few surviving examples. I'm open to various options [...] but we don't have anything formally organised right at this moment. Even though I probably now have the largest collection of de Havilland [Spitfire] propeller parts, I don't have enough undamaged parts to make an entire propeller. I can make a lot of one, but I basically

ABOVE:
'Sandy's' Spitfire is progressing well. With detail work being carried out in the jig, elsewhere skins are being prepared to be fitted later this year. Visible here is the oblique camera door frame, which is beginning to be installed.
AIRFRAME ASSEMBLIES

don't have any blades. There's still time, as I don't need a propeller until about Christmas 2024, so there are still 12-14 months, but it's now towards the top of my list.

"Hopefully, if it's all managed well, by the end of next summer all the internals will come together, serviced and ready to fit into a fuselage that's ready to accept them. Some wings will turn up later on, and the engine will be delivered having been run-in on a stand already. Then it's only down to the propeller. Whilst things have slipped slightly, I'm still confident we'll be airborne in May 2025."

Options are currently being explored for the location of AA810's final assembly. Once that's happened and the aircraft's test-flying is complete, it will not be put out to an existing operator. Rather, Tony Hoskins explains, "We obviously have the charitable aspect of the project which deals with our STEM outreach and our National Monument campaign [see panel at right for details]. We are creating an operating company, the Reconnaissance Heritage Flight, which will be a trading arm of the charity and will have its own supporters' club."

Tony has completed a CAA accountable managers' course, preparing for the Reconnaissance Heritage Flight's establishment.

It will be submitting its own OCM (operational control manual) to the authority during 2024 and plans are well advanced for the training and operations of the aircraft with a very experienced set of pilots.

The expectation is to fly 30-35 hours a year after the busier initial phase in 2025-26, because of what Tony describes as "a huge amount of interest in taking the aeroplane all round Europe, and the world". Possibilities under discussion include ceremonial events in Belgium and the Netherlands, commemorating their reconnaissance pilots, and a return to where AA810 crashed in Norway, with a temporary strip being provided at the village. A US tour has also been mooted, supported by one of the project's commercial partners, as has a trip to New Zealand for Warbirds over Wanaka.

As such a different example of the breed, Spitfire AA810 will certainly not be lacking in global admirers. Through the way in which it's being carried out, it's also a project far removed from most warbird return-to-flight efforts. In every respect, the prospect of this early PR 'Spit' going back to some of its old haunts, and gracing new ones, is a very exciting one. And, step by step, it's getting closer. **A**

For more information, and to support the project, visit www.spitfireaa810.co.uk

IN MEMORIAM

While researching AA810, Tony Hoskins was surprised to discover that there exists no formal, complete roll of honour for all the RAF's units and squadrons which conducted unarmed photographic reconnaissance missions during the Second World War. He's gone a long way towards rectifying that, discovering that 1,570 people from 23 different nations flew such sorties, and that — according to the best figures currently at his disposal — the casualty rate was 53 per cent. Of those, a third are still listed as missing. From this has grown the idea of establishing a National PRU Monument, to be erected at a suitable site in central London. Cross-party support has been promised by 142 MPs, and meetings with the relevant authorities are ongoing. The hope is to achieve an unveiling in August 2025, the same year as AA810's first post-rebuild flight. Donations can be made at www.spitfireaa810.co.uk.

It's now three decades since
the RAF said farewell to its last
'V-bomber', and retired the Victor
K2 tankers of No 55 Squadron.
But they weren't about to slip
quietly away... **WORDS:** BEN DUNNELL

VICTOR
VANQUIS

The 'V-Force' had often been required to adapt. Through major strategic shifts, repeatedly it was reinvented to meet new demands, and so it continued long after the ultimate responsibility of maintaining Britain's nuclear deterrent passed out of RAF hands. Even so, it was incongruous to find one of the final Victors at what had, just a few years before, been a front-line Warsaw Pact air base. If ever an illustration were sought of changing times, there it was, at Hradec Králové in the newly independent Czech Republic during July 1993. It was the second year running that No 55 Squadron had sent one of its veteran tankers to appear in that country, the first having been to Bratislava, then still part of Czechoslovakia, the previous September. What a symbol of détente — and, more than that, of how the 'V-bombers' had been a constant, from having the Eastern Bloc firmly in their bombsights to a new world order, when the last of them helped represent the RAF in a spirit of friendship.

It is now 30 years since the 'V-Force' era came to an end, as No 55 Squadron retired the Victor K2, and with due ceremony. The writing had long been on the wall, and there was to be no stay of execution. Estimates by the Ministry of Defence in the mid-1980s, as it renewed the RAF's strategic tanker force with newly converted VC10s and Tristars, put the Victor's out-of-service date as 1992. In the event, it was only a year later than that. "We always knew", says Tim Butler, a pilot on 55 at the time, "that the Victor wouldn't go on forever."

Yet 1993 was to be no quiet wind-down year. Notions of a post-Cold War 'peace dividend' having been placed on the scrapheap, the crescent-winged leviathans found themselves highly active on multiple fronts. Ever since their considerable success on 1991's Operation 'Desert Storm' — 299 sorties by eight aircraft in the course of the 42-day war — they had been required to support coalition efforts in maintaining no-fly zones over northern and southern Iraq. Then the Balkans flared up, too. Add to those the regular round of training and exercises at home, and there was no question of bowing out with a whimper.

Even so, there were reminders that the Victor was no longer in

➡

MAIN PICTURE;
The three-ship Victor K2 formation mounted for the press on 23 September 1993, XH672, flown by Sqn Ldr Steve Jenkins, leading XL164 and XM717. DENIS J. CALVERT

ABOVE: 'Tanker-tanker' sorties involving one Victor refuelling another were not uncommon.
CROWN COPYRIGHT

BELOW: Scenes from a sortie in XM715 on 15 April 1993, which saw six Tornado GR1s being refuelled. Flt Lt Dave Attwood was in the captain's seat, with Flt Lt Spike Flynn alongside.
DENIS J. CALVERT

the first flush of youth. One of them had turned 1992 into a difficult year. It was on 6 March when, soon after getting airborne from 55's Marham base with an 84,000lb fuel load on board, Flt Lt Tony Ingelbrecht and his crew heard a loud bang. Conducting all the requisite drills, they dumped 50,000lb of the fuel and, just 20 minutes later, landed serial XL190 safely. The problem was traced to the combustion cans on the Rolls-Royce Conway engines, and it proved to be far from isolated. "It is now clear", said the squadron's operations record book entry for

that month, "that combustion cans throughout the fleet are cracking and when the cracks extend too far, the can can burn through". Two engines had been destroyed as a consequence, and at one stage in May 1992 so many Conways had failed inspection that 55 was reduced to just a pair of flyable aeroplanes.

❖

Gradually, the requisite engine work returned more Victors to the line, albeit as the draw-down process started. Tim Butler was

first posted to No 55 Squadron straight from multi-engine training in February 1988, and stayed until the conclusion of the Victor's career. "We did start losing people around mid-'92 as we reduced the number of people on the squadron", he recalls. "It was kind of a managed decline. A fair few of the older AEOs [air electronics officers] and navigators were looking at going into retirement, while the younger crew members were moving off into different roles."

As 1993 dawned, Operation 'Jural' was the overseas focus, this

being the British contribution to enforcement of the southern Iraq no-fly zone. One Victor, XL161, was already there, but on 8 January a second, XL231, was flown out to join it at Muharraq, Bahrain. Apart from RAF Tornado GR1s flying from Dhahran, Saudi Arabia, they supported US Navy assets equipped for probe-and-drogue refuelling: F-14 Tomcats, F/A-18 Hornets, A-6 Intruders and EA-6 Prowlers.

This was a period of heightened tension, with a growing number of Iraqi aerial incursions and the deployment of surface-to-air missiles in the NFZ. Air strikes were mounted on 13 and 18 January, the Victors being in action on both occasions, refuelling coalition aircraft. That month alone the detachment completed 32 'Jural' sorties, totalling 90 hours 50 minutes' flying, this in spite of XL231 suffering engine problems as January came to a close.

The Muharraq deployment went back to being a one-aircraft affair on 6 February, when Tim Butler and his crew ferried XL231 to Britain non-stop. This 'tanker-tanker' sortie involved the other Bahrain-based Victor, and ended at Mildenhall, presumably because Marham's weather was out of limits. Elsewhere, three aircraft detached to Leuchars for the Joint Maritime Course, supporting Tornado F3s, and Exercise 'Northern Banner' saw both air defence and offensive support elements being replenished, among them French Air Force Jaguars. Before departing for Leuchars, a failure on XH672's number two engine control unit surged, in turn damaging the number one ECU. Both powerplants had to be scrapped.

And then there was TANSOR. Long the preserve of the Victor squadrons, this was the air-to-air refuelling element of the UK's quick reaction alert fighter force. Very busy with scrambles during the Cold War years, by 1993 TANSOR — a contraction of 'Tanker Sortie' — had quietened down significantly but was still maintained, albeit now with a "delayed reaction posture", and in alternation with No 101 Squadron's Brize Norton-based VC10 K2/3s. "Basically, it was a week off", says Tim Butler. "You were on three or six hours' readiness, a week at a time, at home ready to be called in. We had a primary and a stand-by crew, and you swapped throughout the day."

Mid-March saw Butler involved in an eventful two-aircraft 'Western Tankex' to the USA. His rendezvous with the other Victor, planned for the 11th, was delayed by 24 hours after he had to turn back to Marham with a low oil pressure indication on one of the engines. Taking on 30,000lb of fuel, he headed for Andrews AFB, Maryland. "We got

caught out in one of the 'storms of the century'", Butler remembers, "me and Sid Buxton. We flew in, landed, and I just remember the weather was horrendous. There were tremendous snows. They declared a state of emergency in Delaware". The storms were associated with Hurricane *Andrew*, and hit the entire eastern seaboard.

"We were supposed to go in and check the aircraft, especially after the winds and the rain, and we eventually managed to get a taxi to take us there, but he was charging us a special emergency rate. We had a ladder to get into the door of the Victor, and normally, once we'd landed and put the aircraft to bed, we left the ladder underneath the nosewheel because there was nowhere else for it to go. This time, there was so much ice around the aircraft that the ladder was covered in it, right up to the little sprockets that came out of the top. The rest of it was under the ice. When we departed on the Monday, we spent a lot of the time just clearing the ice so we could get out from parking and taxi off."

That was nothing compared with what befell XH671. Marham was to host the Queen's RAF 75th anniversary review on 1 April, and while two Victors were detached to Brize Norton for the flypast — cancelled, of course, due to appalling weather — XH671 was to be the static example. In making it look smart, a bomb-aimer's window had just been replaced, after which a pressurisation check was mandated. Suddenly the cabin door blew open, causing quite substantial damage. That was the end of the aircraft's flying life, and it was sold for scrap. >

Long-distance refuelling trails were each given a different codename depending on the aircraft type primarily being supported. Those involving Tornados were dubbed 'Storm' trails, 'Leopard' was used for Jaguars, and 'Hawk' for Harriers. With eight Harrier GR7s and nine Jaguars going trans-Atlantic en route to Gander, Newfoundland, April saw a lot of them, something Tim Butler recalls all too well.

"On 12 April I'd flown out to Goose Bay, taking a 'Hawk' trail of Harriers. We ended up in Goose Bay for four days and got back to the UK on the 16th. On the 19th I was the ground reserve for a 'Leopard' trail, taking Jaguars across to Lajes in the Azores. Basically you had the airborne element, then the reserve for the airborne element and, just in case everything went horribly wrong, they'd get some people in an aircraft as ground reserve, but you'd never get airborne. That was the general plan.

"We were on the ground [...] and we ended up getting launched to go and support the trail because a number of aircraft broke. We went down to Lajes and landed there. On the way, we realised that because we'd never expected to go anywhere, when we'd changed into our immersion suits — and this was true for most of the crew — we'd left everything in the lockers at the squadron. I had with

me an immersion suit and some underwear, and that was it — as had the co-pilot, Paul Ainsworth. The navigator had a NATO travel order; we didn't have an imprest because we were never going to go anywhere. So, we ended up in Lajes with, basically, no clothes and a NATO travel order as our only form of ID.

"From there we went on to St John's, because they'd run out of aircraft [in all, four Victors were involved]. We ended up explaining to a Canadian customs guy about why it was that four guys in slightly smelly clothing only had one bit of paper to identify them. He let us into Canada, and we had to do some clothes shopping in St John's..."

Inevitably there were aircraft issues, some of them minor snags, others more serious. Five planned sorties by the 'Jural' aircraft at Muharraq, XL231, were lost in late June when first its airborne auxiliary powerplant failed, and then it suffered an airbrake hydraulic leak. This was in the midst of a regular airframe rotation, but the incoming Victor, XM715, fared little better. It was put out of action for five days after a fire bottle discharged on start-up. One of three aircraft sent to Leuchars on 14 June for the year's second Joint Maritime Course didn't get back to Marham until 22 September due to unserviceability. At least the planned three-ship formation in the lead of the Queen's

Birthday Flypast went ahead unhindered.

But it would be wrong to paint too negative a picture of Victor availability. These old aeroplanes were still being worked hard, and the groundcrew performed wonders to make it all possible, even if their numbers were cut in June with the disbandment of No 55 Squadron's second-line contingent. "Because we were getting to the end of the aircraft's life", notes Tim Butler, "the spares situation was good, and we still had lots of engineers for a reducing number of aircraft. The ones we had left we were able to keep reasonably serviceable."

'Jural' continued to account for the bulk of 55's flying, two of July's sorties being mounted to support what is described in the squadron record merely as "a Nimrod", but which was in fact an intelligence-gathering No 51 Squadron Nimrod R1. But the expansion of Operation 'Deny Flight', implementation of NATO's no-fly zone over Bosnia and Herzegovina, brought further activity a lot closer to home. On 16 July, a pair of Victors was detailed to assist in the deployment of 12 Jaguars from Coltishall to Gioia del Colle, Italy. Fuel transfers to each

of the six waves were made near Dover, a No 216 Squadron Tristar flying from Milan aiding their later progress.

— ❖ —

A more than interested observer of the Victor force's latter days was John Brown, wing commander STANEVAL (standards and evaluation) within No 38 Group headquarters at Strike Command. His responsibilities covered all the RAF's transport and tanker types, but, having first been posted to Victors as a co-pilot fresh out of training in 1965, he took a special interest in this one. "There was no need, really, from any supervisory or operational point of view to show my face at Marham, but I thought it would be nice for me to do so", he says. "I went three times between December 1992 and August 1993, and flew each time with Paul Millikin [a Victor qualified flying instructor], who was my STANEVAL agent at Marham.

"I declare an interest here: I wanted to go out of nostalgia. I loved the Victor, I loved Marham and I loved everything about air-to-air refuelling. By that time I wasn't going very much higher in the air

force, and I was determined to enjoy my time as wing commander STANEVAL as much as possible. I used to work on the principle that I never stayed at any one location long enough for people to realise why I was there in the first place.

"We did some receiver training, which was very nice because the Victor was much harder than the VC10, so it was good to be able to prove I could still do that. I seem to remember there were many more trim changes in the Victor as you moved to the actual 'in contact' position. The VC10 sat much more easily behind the tanker, and the trim was much more constant throughout. You were OK with the Victor when you were in contact, but it was just the transition that was trickier.

"We had one bizarre moment. We'd briefed that we were going to practise a simulated double engine failure after take-off, which I think we did from relatively light weight. Half-way through the initial actions, a real airframe fire warning light came on. We stopped the drill we were doing and went through the airframe fire drill, by which time the crew had gone very quiet. I was struggling with two of the engines ➋

55 AND '558

No 55 Squadron really was the last bastion of the 'V-Force' within the RAF. Victors aside, it also had 'operational' control of the Vulcan Display Flight, which flew Vulcan B2 XH558 from Waddington. For the crew members involved, many of whom were also drawn from 55, this was a busy spare-time secondary duty. As far as the public was concerned, it all came to an end in September 1992 when XH558 conducted its final performances in RAF hands, the Ministry of Defence having decided to dispose of the aircraft in the face of much furore. But, away from much limelight, the Vulcan did keep on flying while a civilian buyer was sought.

Each month from October 1992 to February 1993, Sqn Ldr Paul Millikin, a Victor QFI on No 55 Squadron, and fellow display captain David Thomas performed short currency sorties lasting half an hour or less, keeping the aircraft active and themselves ready for a delivery flight. "We just used to do circuits at Waddington", Millikin told the author in 2018. "The circuits were very, very tight — full power, wingover, downwind. Good fun."

Eventually, on 18 March the buyer was confirmed as C. Walton Ltd at Bruntingthorpe, its winning bid for the aeroplane £25,000. "I was Victor detachment commander in Bahrain", said Millikin, "and I had a 'phone call from my boss in the UK saying they'd sold the Vulcan and it would be delivered to Bruntingthorpe on 23 March. Would I like to come back and fly it? Well, what do you think? He said, 'We rather thought you might'. He'd booked Jim McDines, another Victor captain, to come and replace me and take over as detachment commander. Unfortunately he could only get me a British Airways

Some of the 1992 Vulcan Display Flight crew. Aircraft captains Dave Thomas and Paul Millikin are respectively third from left and third from right; navigator Al Slack, who assisted a great deal with VDF admin, is second from right, and AEO Barry Masefield at far right.
KEY/DUNCAN CUBITT

first-class ticket back home to London Heathrow, so I had to come back first-class, which was a bit rough..."

The duty was carried out, XH558 leaving Waddington on 23 March, overflying locations around England and Wales, and landing at Bruntingthorpe after a three-hour 25-minute sortie. One 'V-bomber' had, for now, been silenced. It wouldn't be many months before another followed.

at flight idle until reality struck and I was dealing with a real airframe fire whilst simulating asymmetric flight, the aeronautical equivalent of one arm tied behind my back. We went into an emergency visual circuit — too low for the rear crew to abandon the aircraft at that stage. Fortunately the fire light went out, so we continued this circuit. Then, at about 600ft on finals, the bloody light came on again. Well, you could have heard a pin drop in the cockpit. We pressed on and landed, accompanied by the massed ranks of the Marham fire section. Of course it was a spurious warning after all."

The end really was nigh when, on 14 September, the 10-month Bahrain detachment reached its conclusion. No 101 Squadron's VC10s took back the 'Jural' commitment, and Victor XM715 headed home, along with all the equipment and personnel. Make no mistake, however: No 55 Squadron was still very much an active, operational outfit. XL231 engaged in a 'Western Tankex' from 3-7 September, flying to CFB

"NOT A SERIOUS RUNNER"

Air Marshal Sir Brendan 'Benny' Jackson was a Victor man through and through. On his second operational tour, he flew the type as a bomber with No 100 Squadron, experiencing a narrow escape on 20 March 1963 when the Victor B2 on which he was flying as second pilot, XM714, crashed during a night training exercise after entering a spin. Jackson ejected, the only member of the six-man crew to survive. From 1977-79 he was station commander at Marham, by then a tanker base. When No 55 Squadron was into its final year of operations, he was the Air Member for Supply and Organisation at the Ministry of Defence, and had an idea. Ought not a Victor to be retained by the RAF for display purposes? It might, he felt, make a good replacement for the retiring Vulcan.

While sympathetic, the Air Officer Commanding-in-Chief of Strike Command disagreed. Having received a memo from Jackson, ACM Sir John Thomson wrote back on 3 December 1992. "I regret", he said, "that there are sound operational, engineering and financial reasons why I could not recommend taking this matter forward to our colleagues". At a time when the Vulcan was about to be sold with budgetary reasons to the fore, taking on a Victor display aircraft was not a practical proposition. And, Thomson opined, "the weight of public interest in 'V' aircraft has always focused primarily on the Vulcan... I would be surprised if the Victor was regarded as other than a sort of placebo for its demise."

Jackson had "expressed optimism about the Victor's likely display characteristics", but — having sought expert opinion — Thomson didn't share his enthusiasm. "I am advised", he wrote, "that, unfortunately, airframe design limitations would prevent the type of display for which the Vulcan has gained widespread recognition. The Victor tanker version's wings were shortened by some 10 feet compared with the wings of earlier variants in order to reduce wing flexing and resultant fatigue; consequently, the aircraft is less manoeuvrable and would not be able to perform a similar display to the Vulcan... More significantly, the removal of the underwing tanks (a fairly complex engineering task) would in itself lead to increased fatigue consumption. The tanks provide wing-bending moment relief and should not be removed."

Adding in concerns over crew competence and currency, not to mention "the background of RAF redundancies and reduced recruiting", Thomson politely declared the proposal a non-starter. "I regret", he told Jackson, "that I do not see the Victor idea, however laudable in intent, as a serious runner."

Shearwater, Nova Scotia. Eleven sorties were flown for 'Solid Stance', a NATO maritime exercise in the UK's northern waters, and 23 as part of the 'Elder Joust' air defence exercise in which the Victors refuelled RAF fast jets and French Air Force Mirage 2000Ns.

But something of an 'end-of-term' atmosphere began to prevail. September's Battle of Britain 'At Home' Days at Finningley and Leuchars witnessed the last two Victor airshow appearances, on static display both times. They closed a summer in which No 55 Squadron sought to send an aircraft to as many events as could accept a Victor on the ground. Members of the press were taken for flights, and 23 September's air-to-air photo sortie with a Hercules produced some memorable images. A farewell flypast around airfields with a Victor connection took place on the last day of the month, Tony Ingelbrecht and crew doing the honours with XH672.

It looked almost like business as usual on 1 October, as a single Victor conducted a refuelling sortie near the Wash. But that date saw No 55 Squadron being 'down-declared' in its operational role. All that remained were flypast rehearsals, actual flypasts, and delivery flights of those examples destined for preservation. Well, almost all. The disbandment of No 55 Squadron was set for 15 October, and three Victors duly flew past the parade. Behind them came three VC10s, for the unit 'numberplate' was transferred as a reserve identity to No 241 Operational Conversion Unit, the VC10 OCU at Brize Norton. But, before that, a trio of Tornado GR1s "intercepted the Victor formation in the holding pattern and were refuelled simultaneously". You couldn't keep a good tanker down.

———————— ❖ ————————

Still the odd Victor was seen in East Anglian skies, crew currency activities being undertaken by the Victor Disposal Flight as the airframes awaited final disposition. First to go on 19-20 October were two destined for ground instructional use, XL190 to St Mawgan and XL161 to Lyneham. On 11 November, XL164 went to Brize Norton for the same purpose. XM715 flew to Bruntingthorpe on 19 November, bought by the Walton family. It used the callsign 'Meldrew 1', since this was an aircraft with one foot in the grave. Six days later, Tim Butler ferried XL231 to Elvington, home of the Yorkshire Air Museum. It had been privately purchased by Andre Tempest.

"They were a lot of fun", says Butler of these delivery flights. "We had fairly light aircraft because they'd been stripped of quite a lot of the equipment, and no worries about engine life because we generally took off with the lowest possible engine power. Our brief from OC ops at the time, who authorised the sorties, was to take off, do a visual circuit of Marham, fly up the old No 55/57 Squadron line at low-ish level, and then climb away. He asked, 'Did you see the last aircraft do it?' Yes, we had. 'OK, lower and faster than that one.'

"Because the aircraft was so light and we were able to use take-off power, ATC were telling us to stop the climb around flight level 100 or 150, but we couldn't because we were going up so quickly and it was impossible to stop the aircraft climbing. There was a bit of discussion with ATC: 'We'll let you know when we can level off, but it's not going to be for a few thousand feet…'"

Rounding things off, XH672 had the honour of making the last RAF Victor flight, to Shawbury on 30 November, with Handley Page test pilot Johnny Allam on board. Its eventual destination was the then RAF Aerospace Museum at Cosford, where the runway was felt too short for a safe landing. After nearly 40 years, the 'V-Force' had finally met its end. Was it a premature finale? ➡

Tim Butler doesn't think so. "It was the right time for it to go", he states. "I think it would have been hard for it to keep going, because we were struggling with the airspace changes that were coming in. GPS was starting to come in, and we were never going to get it. We were never going to have an updated inertial navigation system, and RVSM [reduced vertical separation minima] we would never have been able to manage either. The equipment was extremely antiquated.

> ❝ *It was a great aircraft to fly, but it was very old and very limited* ❞

"It was a great, fun aircraft to fly, but it was very old and very limited. The Victor was basically a tactical tanker — it burned an awful lot of fuel, but it didn't carry a great deal to start with. Unlike a VC10 or a Tristar, which could do a lot more capability-wise with the fuel they had, we needed an awful lot of Victors to do the same job. It wasn't particularly fast, although we could do things that some fast jets couldn't do, like fly above 40,000ft for extended periods of time at Mach 0.9 if we wanted to. We'd always take the mickey out of Tornado F3 types, with their fighters that couldn't keep up with us.

LAST ON THE LINE

The following eight Victor K2s were flown by No 55 Squadron during 1993, the type's final year of RAF operation. But what were their ultimate fates?

Serial	Name	Aircraft fate
XH671	*Sweet Sue*	Written off at RAF Marham in static cabin pressure test, then scrapped
XH672	*Maid Marian*	Delivered to Shawbury; preserved at RAF Museum Midlands, Cosford
XL161		Instructional airframe at RAF Lyneham, then scrapped
XL164	*Saucy Sal*	Instructional airframe at RAF Brize Norton, then scrapped; nose preserved at Bournemouth Aviation Museum
XL190		Instructional airframe at RAF St Mawgan, then scrapped; nose preserved at RAF Manston History Museum
XL231	*Lusty Lindy*	Preserved at Yorkshire Air Museum, Elvington (taxiable)
XM715	*Teasin' Tina*	Preserved by British Aviation Heritage, Bruntingthorpe
XM717	*Lucky Lou*	Scrapped at RAF Marham; nose preserved at RAF Museum London, Hendon

FINE ART, VICTOR-STYLE

Colourful artwork was a feature of the Victor force in its latter years. XH672 received the name *I Ran Offutt!* on the inside of its crew door, this a reference to an incident on **29 February 1988** when it ran off the runway at Offutt AFB, Nebraska, following a hydraulic failure. *Saucy Sal* (XL164), *Lucky Lou* (XM717) and *Lusty Lindy* (XL231) were, meanwhile, three examples of the nose art applied by No 55 Squadron's Cpl Andy Price during 1991's Gulf War, when the Victor force performed so outstandingly in operating from Muharraq, Bahrain. DENIS J. CALVERT

"But the technology was old, so the crew had to work together a lot more than you do in modern aircraft. There was no punching buttons to go where you needed to go. We didn't have an autopilot linked into the navigation system; the only way of navigating was by us selecting a heading and the navigator telling us which way to go. We had very good crew relationships and crew camaraderie.

"The ethos of the squadron was very much that we would do whatever was needed to sort the fighters out. This is me speaking as a Victor guy — I'm sure VC10 guys would say differently — but we were always led to believe we were the preferred tanker, because we tended to stretch ourselves a bit further to get the fighters where they needed to go. We'd take them that extra mile, just because, I guess, we had guys who had been on the force a very long time, and that was the ethos. And we looked the part as a tactical aeroplane. It wasn't a converted airliner, it was a converted bomber, and we wanted to be a tactical-type force.

"When I got posted, it was the worst thing in the world to go to Victors. Who wanted to go to that squadron of ageing aircraft, down at Marham in the middle of nowhere? But the fact that we were working with fast jet aircraft all the time, and we were really part of that fast jet family, was so much fun. And the Victor definitely played a really great role in the air force." 

BELOW: Drag 'chute streamed, obviously in a bit of a crosswind, XH672 rolls out. DENIS J. CALVERT

WHEN EAGLE DARED

Beginning 75 years ago, the story of British Eagle is typical of many a British independent airline — a popular venture done down by government policy. The late Bruce Hales-Dutton looked back to a 2009 interview with Eagle's founder Harold Bamberg to chart this much-loved carrier's rise and fall

WORDS: BRUCE HALES-DUTTON

The first day of 1964, and Britannia 312 G-AOVT *Enterprise* comes in to land at Liverpool's Speke airport. KEN FIELDING

I f you thought low-cost air travel started with Ryanair and easyJet, think again. Michael O'Leary and Stelios Haji-Ioannou weren't even born when the British air transport industry took its first steps towards the freedom of choice and lower fares today's passengers enjoy.

It was on 6 June 1953 that the first post-war scheduled international flight to be undertaken by a British independent carrier took off for Belgrade. Until then, government policy meant scheduled operations could only be conducted by the two nationalised airlines, British Overseas Airways Corporation and British European Airways.

The operator of that flight was British Eagle, founded by Harold Bamberg. From then on, the astute and persistent Bamberg was able gradually to create a network of scheduled domestic and European services, as well as carving out a niche market in the Caribbean. It also operated charter services and, indeed, Bamberg claimed to be the "creator of the package tour business."

Certainly, no airline boss in Britain worked harder to cut the cost of air travel than Harold Bamberg. He brought competition to the industry and raised service standards. He was a pioneer of international regional air services and helped open up both domestic trunk routes and trans-Atlantic operations to independent airlines. Within 20 years British Eagle had become Britain's biggest privately owned airline. But that didn't prevent its sudden financial collapse under the weight of a deadly combination of adverse economic conditions, official intransigence and the hostility of the two flag-carriers.

All that was more than half a century ago. British Eagle and Harold Bamberg are virtually forgotten today. Yet he was a larger-than-life character who lived well, drove around in a chauffeur-driven car complete with telephone, dictating machine and personalised numberplate, and played polo with Prince Philip at Windsor Great Park.

Harold Rolf Bamberg was born on 17 November 1923 in Berlin, to a family whose circumstances he later described as "comfortable". Soon they moved to the UK, and Harold left school at 17 to join the RAF, in which he learned to fly. After the war he planned a career in aviation, and for a time worked for American Overseas Airlines. He registered Eagle Aviation in April 1948 as an air charter operation with capital of £100. He was just 25. The new airline's name was chosen with care. "I think birds are wonderful, particularly the eagle", Bamberg told the author in a 2009 interview. "It has such an incredible wing."

Eagle's first aircraft was a converted Handley Page Halifax VIII, G-AJBL. "We flew fruit from Italy and Spain for Covent Garden merchants", Bamberg recalled. The first flight carried a cargo of cherries from Verona to Bovingdon. A second Halifax, G-ALEF, was acquired in the all-over red livery of its previous owner, Vingtor Airways of Norway. Inevitably, given the scheme, it was christened *Red Eagle*.

The Air Ministry awarded the new airline a contract for regular flights during the Berlin Airlift. The two Halifaxes were based at Fuhlsbüttel near Hamburg and in February 1949 were joined by two further aircraft. All four flew around the clock until civilian operations ended in August 1949 when *Red Eagle*, commanded by Capt J. W. 'Pancho' Villa, flew the airline's final mission of the airlift. Together, the Halifaxes carried more than 7,000 tons of cargo in 1,054 sorties and logged a combined total of over 545 flying hours. They then returned to the UK to take up residence at Aldermaston, Berkshire.

Participation in the airlift was one of several things Bamberg had in common with fellow airline entrepreneur Freddie Laker. But Bamberg denied it had been a lucky break. "If we hadn't joined

> ## 66 *If we hadn't joined the airlift we'd have been requisitioned* 99

we'd have been requisitioned", he insisted. "The trouble was we went for some months without agreeing how much we should be paid. One day I went to a meeting with the government. They said, 'How much do you want?' I said we wanted cost plus 12.5 per cent. They thought it was quite reasonable. People think we made lots of money out of it, but we didn't."

ABOVE:
In front of a BAC One-Eleven, Harold Bamberg addresses British Eagle's creditors during a meeting held on 20 November 1968 in a Heathrow hangar.
ALAMY

After the Halifaxes came the Avro Yorks, of which Eagle was eventually to acquire a fleet of 11. In 1949 Bamberg announced the airline had agreed to buy three aircraft from BOAC. John Sauvage, whose distinguished war record included a spell as Lord Mountbatten's pilot in the Far East, was appointed chief pilot of the York fleet. The aircraft quickly proved their worth by carrying a wide variety of cargo, probably the most spectacular being a 19ft-long ship's propeller shaft weighing in excess of nine tons.

By 1951, the airline had been awarded regular government trooping contracts and was employing 100 people including 12 pilots. But although the regulatory climate was improving under the new Conservative government, the independent carriers were still limited to ad hoc operations, with scheduled services remaining the province of the state-owned airlines.

"I thought that any businessman who tried to tangle with the government or state airlines should have his brains tested", Bamberg later told journalist Roger Bray, ➋

It was Viking 1 G-AKBH which, on 6 June 1953, operated Eagle Airways' inaugural scheduled service, from Blackbushe via Munich to Belgrade. The aircraft was photographed at Heathrow six years later. ADRIAN M. BALCH COLLECTION

Eagle Aviation's first aircraft, Halifax VIII G-AJBL, being loaded with supplies at Wunstorf for a Berlin Airlift mission. GETTY

DC-3 G-AMYB was the longest-serving example of the type with Eagle, being on strength for four years. This shot was taken at Heathrow in 1956, during which year the machine was also leased to BEA. BOB O'BRIEN COLLECTION

co-author of *Flight to the Sun*, the story of the holiday revolution. Uncharacteristically disheartened, he sold the Yorks to rival operator Skyways and considered packing up. He was, however, persuaded to carry on by colleagues, particularly John Sauvage who was now operations director, and was later to run Britannia Airways and the Thomson Travel Group.

Bamberg did continue and with renewed vigour, acquiring the inevitable Douglas DC-3s, and a fleet of twin-engine Vickers Vikings. "I had 22", he recalled. "I bought 37 from BEA and sold the other 15 to other operators". Now he needed to find work for them. Persistent lobbying by Bamberg and others resulted in new government regulations, which allowed the independent airlines to apply for scheduled licences as long as their operations didn't overlap those of BEA and BOAC. Eagle was granted a seven-year licence to operate scheduled flights from London to Belgrade via Munich, thus inaugurating air links between the UK and Yugoslavia. Departing from Blackbushe on 6 June 1953, it was Viking G-AKBH which had the honour of performing the first post-war international scheduled flight by a British independent airline.

❖

That October, now retitled as Eagle Airways, the carrier launched its second scheduled service, to Aalborg and Gothenburg. Advertising for its twice-weekly Scandinavian operation featured the reigning Miss Sweden.

Bamberg's next move was to create what he claimed was virtually a new market. "In 1954", he said, "we persuaded the Ministry of Aviation about a concept we called 'the jockey and the horse': the travel agent was the jockey and the horse was the airline". Permission was eventually granted for a limited programme, but Bamberg was rebuffed when he tried to find a suitable 'jockey'. Thomas Cook was "not interested in low-cost air travel", so Bamberg bought the Sir Henry Lunn company in 1955, later acquiring Poly Travel and forming Lunn-Poly.

"There was a licensing system introduced in the low-fare element", Bamberg recounted. "In other words, it was the package holiday business which we innovated". He wasn't the only operator to make a similar claim. Roger Bray commented, "It's always been a moot point about what is a package holiday but Bamberg was probably the first to combine the roles of tour operator and airline under one roof."

The first flights were to Italy and Spain, advertised as tours under the names 'Treasures of Italy' and 'Castles in Spain'. "They were very tiring but the clients loved them", Bamberg told the author. "The Vikings were noisy brutes which flew at 200mph". Majorca — a four-hour flight — was added later. Pilots also had their reservations about the Viking. "It was a pig!" remarked Capt Ralph Kohn, who started as an Eagle first officer. "It was difficult to land because you had to three-point it."

Soon, holidays were available on the never-never. Hire-purchase facilities offered by Lunn-Poly made buying travel, according to Bamberg's publicity, "as easy as buying a radio set on credit". By 1957 Eagle was offering summer flights to Perpignan with coach connections to the Costa Brava for £32.50 on Mondays or £36 at weekends. The 'King's Flight' inclusive holiday programme promised a 15-day package to Majorca, promising "all the magic of swift comfortable travel in gleaming Viking 'planes". The cost was just £40.

Eagle took another notable step forward in 1957 when it acquired its first turbine-powered aircraft, Viscount 800 G-APDW. The Viscount offered levels of passenger comfort

> ## 66 *The licensing system was not in favour of private companies* 99

well above those of the Viking. Over the next decade the airline would operate a mix of leased and owned Series 700s and 800s. "We achieved all this", Bamberg said, "but the British licensing system was not and could not be in favour of private companies, and the state airlines were protected."

Even though he was soon introducing new scheduled services from Manchester to Basle, Hamburg and Copenhagen, Bamberg was still frustrated by the near-monopoly enjoyed by the state corporations. As a result, he decided to begin Caribbean operations from a base in Bermuda. It was his biggest gamble yet. Two Viscount 800s were ordered from Vickers, and by the end of the year the Bermudan government had granted permission for up to 28 services a week between the colony and New York and Montreal.

BOAC was already serving the Bermuda-New York route but British Eagle's intervention boosted Britain's share of total traffic. Within a year Eagle had pushed its network to Montreal, Baltimore and Washington as well as Nassau. Sales offices were opened in key north American cities. It was the first time a British independent carrier had gone head-to-head with BOAC.

Eagle was now reorganised into what was essentially a group. A new company, Eagle Airways (Bermuda), was formed to fly the scheduled Viscount services, while another ❯

CAMERA WORK

The York freighters weren't the only Avro 'heavies' to enter the Eagle fleet. In mid-October 1955, Lancaster VII NX739 arrived at Blackbushe on loan from the Ministry of Supply, with a very specific purpose in mind: use as an aerial photographic platform, its gun turrets modified with Perspex. While it retained its military serial and markings, it was flown by Eagle Aviation crews, and carried the company's logo. Duties included acting as an air-to-air photo-ship for ministry photographers to capture official images during the 1956 Farnborough show, while *Flight*'s lensmen used it in the same role at other times. NX739 was retired in January 1957, departing to Wroughton for scrapping. It was a sad fate for what is believed to have been the last ex-No 617 Squadron Lancaster in flying condition. To replace it, the ministry made available Lincoln B2 RF332 for Eagle's use. At one stage the fake squadron codes 'EA-S', standing for Eagle Aviation Services, were added. However, the Lincoln's assignment was fairly short-lived, the aircraft being returned to the military in May 1958.
Ben Dunnell

Lincoln RF332 with the Eagle logo on its nose. TONY CLARKE COLLECTION

RIGHT:
Unusual company for an Eagle Airways Viscount, as VR-BAY, a Series 805, sits at New York's Idlewild airport between services to Bermuda.
ADRIAN M. BALCH COLLECTION

subsidiary handled aircraft servicing and operations in the Caribbean.

"We started flying London-Miami", Bamberg recalled to the author, "but we had to fly London-Bermuda, Bermuda-Nassau and Nassau-Miami so we had two stops on the way. BOAC said there was no traffic to Miami. We disagreed and we were proved right. We ran a shuttle between Nassau and Miami with Viscount aircraft four times a day and we ran a shuttle between Bermuda and New York three times a day. So we opened up the Caribbean quite extensively."

For its longer flights the airline was now operating piston-engine DC-6s, eventually building up a fleet of six. "I bought three from the US", Bamberg recalled. "In the early days we couldn't buy American aircraft because we weren't allowed the dollars". The first two were acquired from the American carrier Slick Airways. In Eagle service they were known as 'Eaglemasters'. After conversion from cargo to passenger-carrying configuration the first DC-6 entered service in November 1958. The aircraft would be employed on a variety of tasks, from passenger charters to fulfilling government trooping contracts. And they were worked hard. In its first year, G-APOM flew a staggering total of 3,804 hours.

Two DC-6s were swapped in 1964 for three ex-Saudi Arabian Airlines C-54s, specifically for high-density inclusive tour operations following Eagle's acquisition of Liverpool-based Starways. Eagle also inherited Starways' lucrative domestic network and five of its C-54 pilots. The operation was renamed British Eagle (Liverpool). IT holiday flights with C-54s were based at Liverpool and Manchester, supplemented by ad hoc charters. Former Starways pilot Capt Feenan commanded Eagle's first holiday charter from Manchester, bound for Palma, in May 1964. In the last two weeks of July the C-54s operated six round trips between Glasgow and Tarbes, France for the Lourdes pilgrimage. But the remaining DC-6 fleet was struggling to handle the volume of work involved in a government contract for flights between the UK and Australia in support of ballistic missile testing at Woomera.

Meanwhile, in a typically bold and innovative move, Bamberg unveiled his very low fares concept. It had been carefully thought out: to avoid having to seek approval from foreign governments, and the inevitable objections of their carriers, it was intended to apply only to routes between the UK and colonial destinations. An application was made to the Air Transport Advisory Council in 1958 and resulted in its longest ever hearing.

Eagle proposed, for example, to fly to Malta for £19 compared with BEA's £52.60, and to Singapore for £199 when BOAC wanted £351. Also included were services to the Bahamas and the Caribbean, East and West Africa, Cyprus and Gibraltar. The bid ultimately failed, but there was no question that Bamberg was the first to offer scheduled tickets at a fraction of state airline fares.

During a February 1958 debate in the House of Commons, William Shepherd, the Conservative MP for Cheadle, made a point of highlighting an airline which, he said, "has done more to bring about cheap fares and to bring new ideas to the industry". According to Shepherd, "Eagle Airways has started with the idea of providing an all-in holiday for almost as low a cost as the price of an ordinary ticket for the air journey". He added: "I'm convinced that a public corporation would never have conceived this idea. There would have been a dozen ways why it was impracticable to do it."

Indeed, BEA, which was facing a £284,000 annual loss, refused to believe Eagle could operate services economically. "Sooner or later", the state-owned carrier predicted, "they will come back for a fare increase."

Predictably, the nationalised airlines' objections were upheld but the government found itself forced into a compromise which allowed Eagle to launch a service from London to Nassau via Bermuda in conjunction with BOAC. The corporation was strongly opposed, but the deal did allow Eagle to offer a monthly low-fare Skycoach flight as well as a weekly first and economy service. In return, Eagle agreed to drop its outstanding VLF applications.

Skycoach services between London and Bermuda started in October 1960, the year Eagle moved its base from Blackbushe to Heathrow. Bamberg told *Flight* that the airline could boast "the largest British network of independent scheduled services in Europe". It had, he said, "tried desperately to get a decent scheduled pattern". European routes, he went on, broke even in 1959 and "should show a profit in 1960". Bamberg added, "We see our future largely in terms of international scheduled flying, both passengers and freight. Trooping, charter and inclusive tour work don't lend themselves to planning ahead."

Then came major change. In 1960 a controlling stake in Eagle was acquired by the Cunard Steamship Company. Bamberg explained, "Lord Brocklebank [Cunard's chairman] came into my office complete with bowler hat and umbrella saying he wanted to talk to me. About a million people a year crossed the Atlantic by air and they knew the day of regular crossings by the big boats was virtually over. Cunard wanted to follow the other shipping companies and get into the aviation business. We did a deal and I became the aviation director of Cunard. They needed good management."

BOAC was also losing money. "The culture was one of trade unionism and they were losing the British share. We had the opportunity, with the minister's blessing, to join up with Cunard, which, by that time had bought 60 per cent of Eagle."

The resulting £30-million company, known as Cunard Eagle, applied to fly scheduled services across the north Atlantic and secured the right to operate one flight a day. Initially, Britannias were used but they were to be replaced by Boeing 707s. Two Rolls-Royce-powered 707-465s were ordered in 1961 and registered G-ARWD and G-ARWE. True to form, BOAC appealed, citing its order for 45 VC10s and a promise by the aviation minister that there would be no other British competitor on the route. It was a stunning blow to Cunard Eagle.

But although BOAC had won its appeal it was still not satisfied. "Its chairman, Sir Matthew Slattery, contacted Brocklebank wanting to do a deal with him and get rid of us", Bamberg said. "They made a very strong proposition."

The fact was that BOAC had considered the combination of Cunard and Eagle too much of a threat to its position in the North Atlantic market. Secret negotiations resulted in the corporation taking a 70 per cent stake in what would be known as BOAC-Cunard.

Bamberg had been kept in the dark. "I was consulted at the very end. A lot of it was done under cover. Cunard actually did a deal to form another £30-million company with 10 Boeings on the north Atlantic. They were offered a controlling interest but Brocklebank didn't want that. He settled for a third. Our Boeings were transferred to BOAC-Cunard."

The result was to reduce Eagle to a shadow of its former self. It had been stripped of its best routes and left with a top-heavy engineering organisation which had been geared up to operate the big jets. Bamberg soon lost patience with the new set-up. "The tea and biscuits were all right, but when it came to management it wasn't my cup of tea. I didn't agree with their culture". He resigned and subsequently ➤

bought back what was left of his company.

The early months of 1963 saw a struggle for survival. Now, as British Eagle International Airlines, it was making a loss but was beginning its climb back to profitability. Within the next two years its fleet would include seven Viscount 700s and 17 Britannia 300s. In fact, the Britannia fleet was to be a key element in Eagle's recovery. It was to operate 23 Series 300 examples and the first, a Series 318, had been leased from the Cuban national airline Cubana. Registered G-APYY, it entered service with Eagle in April 1960 on a government charter to Christmas Island as part of the nuclear test programme. A second Britannia arrived in 1963.

And with expansion plans now well-advanced, Eagle began looking for more. The newly acquired examples included seven ex-BOAC Series 312s. Two Series 308s, previously owned by collapsed Argentinean carrier Transcontinental, were converted to freighter configuration, a complex task which created virtually new aircraft capable of carrying 132 passengers or 36,000lb of cargo. This notably enabled them to take over from the DC-6s on military freight runs to Australia in respect of weapons trials.

The Britannias undertook a varied programme of flying from Heathrow that included scheduled services to European destinations

and government charters, as well as package holiday flights to Europe, North Africa and the Caribbean. British Eagle extended its network in 1963 by launching operations from London to Glasgow, Edinburgh and Belfast, ending BEA's 18-year monopoly. The Britannias were operating in competition with BEA's Vanguards.

"There were a lot of complaints about BEA's service", Bamberg remembered. "We offered hot breakfasts, trickle loading and a lot of other minor innovations in terms of public service". Liverpool was later added to the list of domestic destinations. BEA's opposition was to some extent tempered by the restrictions applied to Eagle's licences which limited the frequency of services. The national airline's load factors were barely affected as Bamberg continued to press for an easing of the restrictions.

The inaugural service, to Glasgow in November, was followed by operations to Edinburgh and Belfast. BEA responded by 'sandwiching' the newcomer's services. "It was quite scandalous what they got up to", fumed Eagle's archivist and historian, former avionics engineer Eric Tarrant. "The great thing was that we raised the standard, and that was acknowledged in Parliament."

In 1963, British Eagle moved from the Marble Arch Air Terminal and transferred passenger check-in facilities to the Knightsbridge

Air Terminal, which was closer to Heathrow. By the middle of the decade, Eagle was offering scheduled services to nine destinations in the UK, Channel Islands and Ireland, and 11 in mainland Europe.

What Bamberg described in the airline's staff newspaper as "a big step for us" came in 1965 with the arrival of the first of an eventual seven BAC One-Elevens. British Eagle's inaugural One-Eleven service, from London to Glasgow, was performed in May 1966 by Series 200 G-ATTP leased from Zambia Airways. It had become the first British carrier to fly jets on domestic services.

With the arrival of another Series 200, British Eagle expanded its One-Eleven operations, inaugurating in quick succession services to Tunis and Djerba, Luxembourg and Stuttgart, and Dinard and La Baule. By July One-Elevens had been introduced on scheduled flights to Liverpool, Newquay, Palma, Perpignan, Pisa and Rimini. Three Series 300s were leased from the Kuwait Finance Company and two acquired from the manufacturer. The aircraft were also used on IT charters to Mediterranean resorts from London and Manchester on behalf of Lunn-Poly, Everyman and Global Holidays.

The 'Super One-Eleven', as British Eagle called it, was well-liked by both passengers and crew. Ralph Kohn was one of the pilots. "The One-Eleven was my first jet", he said. "I transferred to it from Britannias. It was great fun. We went to resorts like Pisa and Rimini. I can also remember flying to Djerba."

But the big turboprops still ruled the long-haul routes. British Eagle

> ## 66 *Eagle overtook BUA as Britain's largest independent airline* 99

made history in 1966 when Capt J. Gerrish commanded a Britannia on the first direct commercial flight from Africa to South America, taking nine-and-three-quarter hours. The return, from Recife to Windhoek, took 12 hours. Average speed in both directions was 350mph. The same year, a British Eagle Britannia completed a 26,000-mile round-the-world charter flight with visits to eight countries.

The airline was growing strongly now. In 1967 the *Economist* reported

Eagle had overtaken British United Airways as Britain's largest independent airline following a period of "impressive growth". The journal added, "British Eagle increased its capacity five-fold in five years". It offered nearly one-third of the available independent airline capacity.

Yet its days were numbered. Harold Wilson's Labour government favoured the independent airlines even less than its predecessors. Sterling had been devalued and a £50 limit had been slapped on the amount of cash Britons could take abroad. The trooping contracts were ebbing away too. The final straw came when BOAC called for British Eagle's licence to fly Caribbean charters to be revoked because of "irregularities."

The Air Transport Licensing Board, successor to ATAC, threw out BOAC's case but upheld its subsequent appeal. The nationalised airline had left the board "in no doubt" that British Eagle had abused the terms and conditions of its inclusive tour licence by advertising it as "little different from a scheduled service."

Meanwhile, British Eagle had agreed terms to acquire a pair of ex-Qantas 707-138s just before the collapse. Matters weren't helped when representatives of the

ABOVE:
A rare publicity shot of Cunard Eagle Boeing 707-465 VR-BBW (later G-ARWD) on its first flight to the Bahamas in March 1962.
AIRTEAMIMAGES.COM COLLECTION

Viking G-AHPO in military colours as XF631 for trooping purposes. EAGLE ARCHIVE

SUPER TROOPERS

British government trooping contracts were very lucrative for Eagle. In 1954 it was awarded a two-year, £1.25-million deal to take troops and their dependents to Cyprus, Gibraltar, Malta, Libya and the Canal Zone, known as the Med Air contract. A number of Vickers Vikings, with temporary military serials applied, were based at Nicosia and used on flights to British bases in the Middle East, North Africa and Aden. When in 1956 a contract was won to serve West Africa, the Vikings operated a weekly service via Gibraltar, though the type's short range and low speed meant the round trip could last at least eight days.

More modern equipment came with the DC-6s. Two of them serviced a new trooping contract to Nairobi and Aden, being equipped with 98 rearward-facing seats in line with policy for such flights. That finished in 1959, but then

Eagle was awarded a tender to perform the British courier service to Australia in connection with weapons trials, not least those of the Blue Steel stand-off bomb, flying to Woomera and, if necessary, Adelaide. Passenger/freight-configured DC-6s were allocated, and G-ARZO set off from Heathrow for the first such flight on 8 June 1962.

When the Britannias became available from late 1963, they started taking over; the Bristol aircraft were also used on trooping runs to Singapore and Hong Kong. To provide them with the obligatory rear-facing seats, the existing seats were simply turned backwards. But an offer from Caledonian to use Boeing 707s on the Singapore route saw the Scottish charter operator gain the contract in December 1967, and begin operations the following April. This was one of the setbacks that ultimately clipped Eagle's wings.

owners, Kleinwort Benson, and British Eagle's bankers, Hambros, left a meeting with aviation minister Roy Jenkins in a gloomy frame of mind. "He said there was no future for the independent airlines", Bamberg recalled. "It wasn't surprising they got cold feet". The 707-138s passed to Laker Airways, while a pair of -365s ordered direct from Boeing in 1966 weren't delivered.

The summer operation proceeded as planned despite the cancellation of inclusive tour bookings worth more than £1 million. In October 1968 the company's management initiated a comprehensive across-the-board economy drive in consultation with the bankers. Redundancy notices went out to over 400 staff in London and Liverpool. The Liverpool maintenance base was closed. These measures produced a cut of 14 per cent in total staff numbers.

By the end of October Eagle had finalised a new deal with its bankers. But within days — and without warning — the airline's IT licences to Bermuda and the Bahamas were revoked after further objections from BOAC. Although these services represented just three per cent of the 1969 flying programme, it was enough to scare the banks, which withdrew their support. With no sources of finance to tide the airline over the lean winter season, the end was in sight. Bamberg refused to give up the fight, and approached the government for assistance. It was a forlorn hope.

❖

On 6 November the British Eagle board announced the imminent cessation of all flying. This sent shockwaves rippling through the industry and came as a bombshell to the 2,500 staff. "The first thing I knew was when a notice went up in the hangar saying the company was ceasing operations at midnight", said Eric Tarrant.

"I had no suspicions at all", recalled Ralph Kohn. "I was due to fly that evening on a One-Eleven to Khartoum or Cairo. One of my friends told me, 'You're not going anywhere. The airline's gone bust'. We then heard it via the BBC."

All but two of the airline's aircraft had returned to their UK bases by the end of the day. The last-but-one to arrive was Britannia freighter G-AOVM with a cargo of oranges from Israel. The final Eagle service

Appropriately enough registered G-ARMY, a British Eagle DC-6A sits at Adelaide in November 1963 with freight doors open while engaged in weapons testing support work. ADRIAN M. BALCH COLLECTION

was flown by Britannia G-AOVG and commanded by Capt Bishop. It had been operating a charter flight from Heathrow to Suriname via Rotterdam. Until the return journey, when the aircraft made a refuelling stop in the Azores, the Britannia's crew had been blissfully unaware of the airline's collapse. At the airport they found a telex message on the handling agents' desk from Pan American. It read, "British Eagle International Airlines ceased trading at 16:30 11/7/68", adding ominously, "All credit facilities withdrawn."

The Britannia's crew hastily hid the message, which airport staff obviously hadn't yet seen because the aircraft was allowed to proceed unhindered. It was a different story at Rotterdam. Immediately the Britannia arrived on the apron the airport manager appeared on the flight deck to impound it by chaining the throttles to the control column with a large padlock. Following some delicate negotiations with the Dutch charterer, which agreed to pay the outstanding bills, the chains were removed and the aircraft was allowed to leave.

Meanwhile, Bamberg was issuing a notice to staff in which he told them, "Your actions have been observed by the whole nation with astonishment". A skeleton staff was retained to assist the receivers in winding up the company, while a small group of engineers stayed on to ensure the aircraft were fit for sale. At that time the fleet comprised 27 aeroplanes: 13 Britannias, seven One-Elevens, three Viscounts and a Dove. The hangars and offices were closed on 8 November. There wasn't enough space to park the aircraft at Heathrow, so some had to be dispersed to locations like Luton.

Following the closure, the Eagle board issued a statement blaming the collapse on the devaluation of sterling, the £50 travel allowance and the prevailing economic situation that had triggered a severe recession in the holiday

---

---

travel market. The airline failed with debts of £5.5 million and there was criticism of the ATLB and its predecessor, ATAC. Ironically, it had been Eagle's very low fares proposal which had highlighted the lack of official powers to deal with the situation.

At around this time, the Edwards Committee was taking evidence for its inquiry into the future of British air transport. Later it recommended the formation of an independent body to handle the industry's safety and economic regulation, leading to the formation in 1972 of the Civil Aviation Authority.

At the age of 45 Harold Bamberg was young enough to put his energies into other enterprises. As the UK distributor for Beechcraft he would claim to have sold 1,000 aircraft before retreating to his Surrey farm to breed bloodstock. He died on 28 September 2022, aged 98.

Like Sir Freddie Laker, Bamberg cast a giant shadow over the industry. But Eric Tarrant believes there were significant differences between them. "Laker was very hands-on while Bamberg was concerned about the whole industry and seeing that the independent airlines got a fair crack of the whip. He was a great character and very much respected by Eagle people."

The book value of the airline's assets might have been put at more than £5 million, but the liquidators appointed to salvage as much as possible for creditors didn't realise anything like it. Part of the problem was the large number of Britannias already on the market as airlines transitioned to jets. The creditors included Rolls-Royce (£630,000), Esso (£300,000), Elliot (£36,000), Dunlop (£30,000) and Vickers (£10,000). Staff were way down the list, and it wasn't until 1977 that a final distribution was made.

Eric Tarrant received a cheque for 46p. It was just enough for a pint of beer to toast the passing of what one industry observer called "a substantial portion of the British air transport industry." Ⓐ

ABOVE:
It was a tough task for British Eagle to take on BEA, from which a Comet 4 and a Trident are visible behind One-Eleven 301AG G-ATPJ on the Glasgow apron in mid-June 1967.
BOB O'BRIEN COLLECTION

NEVER SAY NEVER...

Nobody told the Historic Aircraft Preservation Society it couldn't have a Lancaster flown back to the UK from Australia, and operate it in private hands — so, it did. It left an outstanding legacy, for the 'Lanc' now known as *Just Jane* probably wouldn't otherwise survive. How did some of the key players in the project view it? **WORDS:** BEN DUNNELL

The fruit of many labours: Lancaster VII NX611 runs up its four Merlins during one of just two flying display appearances it made in HAPS hands, at Blackbushe in September 1967. RICHARD HITCHENS

ABOVE:
A memorable scene from the Lancaster's delivery flight, as an escort is provided by Royal Australian Air Force Canberra B20 A84-307 from No 2 Squadron and No 57 Squadron, RAF Victor B1 XH591 at the start of the leg between RAAF Butterworth, Malaysia, and Calcutta on 6 May 1965. CROWN COPYRIGHT

'If you don't ask, you don't get'. For the Historic Aircraft Preservation Society, that mantra proved both a blessing and a curse. When it wrote to the French government asking for an Avro Lancaster, little did it know it might actually be given one. But, despite the considerable ordeals that followed, thank goodness it was. Without that eager — inspired, naïve, call it what you will — intervention, we wouldn't now be anticipating the moment when NX611 flies again.

When it takes to the air at East Kirkby, on current timescales it will be doing so for the first time in almost 60 years. Had things turned out more positively in this Lancaster's previous airworthy life, we'd be looking at a different story. The career of NX611 with HAPS and subsequent operator Reflectaire is a tale very much of its time, when groups of well-meaning preservation pioneers sought to save what they could, even as flyers, on a relative shoestring, calling in help and favours from all quarters to make up for what they lacked in money. Sometimes it worked, sometimes it didn't. Yet the debt owed to those who made it happen in the first place is considerable.

Young enthusiast Bill Fisher was no stranger to letter-writing. He'd asked the Cranfield College of Aeronautics for Corsair IV KD431, to be kept with the then nascent Fleet Air Arm Museum at Yeovilton, and been given it! Founding HAPS with a group of like-minded individuals such as Russ Snadden — later best-known for his restoration of Messerschmitt Bf 109 G-2/Trop 'Black 6' — Bernard Clarkson, Brian Arbery and others made the requests sound more official, yet those to the Soviet ambassador in London for a MiG-15, and to the US Air Force for a U-2, understandably fell on deaf ears. The missive to the French was another matter. Yes, they said, HAPS could have a Lancaster. But Bill admits he had no idea the Aéronautique Navale based its 'Lanc' fleet not in northern France, but the South Pacific territory of New Caledonia. That was until he read the response that arrived on his parents' doormat, saying the aeroplane could be delivered from Nouméa to either Australia or New Zealand. What to do now?

The answer: call Sir Roy Dobson, former Avro leading light, now of Hawker Siddeley. Fisher did so from work at insurance brokers Holmwoods, Back and Manson, where he was a clerk. Having explained the situation to a lady at the other end of the line, she asked where he could be contacted. Bill replied, "Holmwoods, the Lloyd's brokers", leading to the misapprehension that he was either a Lloyd's 'name' or a senior figure in the organisation. Whatever, it did the trick. Dobson arranged for Hawker de Havilland to accept the aircraft at Bankstown, Sydney, and generously donated £10,000 towards the flight home.

The hand-over of serial WU-15, the former NX611, took place on 13 August 1964, and attendant publicity brought its own benefits. A Sydney solicitor, Bruce Miles, offered to help. He put together the crew and made the trip financially viable, both through selling seats and sourcing sponsorship. That backing came primarily from a fast-growing Queensland resort, hence the name applied to the aircraft, *Spirit of Surfers Paradise*. ➲

ABOVE:
Made it! As per the schedule, the 'Lanc' arrived at Biggin Hill on 13 May 1965, ready to star in the Air Fair static display.
DENIS J. CALVERT

Already a British home for the Lancaster had been settled. Biggin Hill was a regular spotting haunt for Bill Fisher and other HAPS founders, and the civil side of the airfield was being built up by Jock Maitland and Ted Drewery. What's more, their plan was for an aviation museum to be founded there. Maitland, Fisher has written, "was another of those who worked behind the scenes to get the aircraft home". With him it was arranged for the 'Lanc' to arrive on 13 May 1965, opening day of the Biggin Hill Air Fair.

That schedule was fixed with Maitland eight months in advance. Given the vicissitudes of old aeroplanes, that it was adhered to is remarkable. Touchdown at Biggin duly took place mid-afternoon on the appointed date. The 19-day, 70-flying hour journey had gone swimmingly. It was, all told, a great achievement. As Fisher wrote, the aircraft was, "registered to Russ and I as G-ASXX, flown by a crew of Australians, who may or may not have had British licences endorsed for the Lancaster, carrying a full complement of occupants, every available seat having been sold, and with an airworthiness document which, on detailed inspection, might not have been accepted at an international civil airport."

The authorities may have turned the odd blind eye up to this point, but no longer. As part of the deal with the Air Registration Board whereby a certificate of airworthiness was issued for the ferry flight, G-ASXX could no longer be flown. Walk-throughs raised money, and HAPS attracted new members. A team from Field Aircraft Services at Heathrow came over to perform maintenance, and some engine runs were carried

> **❝ I selected wheels and flaps down — I needed high drag, and quickly ❞**

out. These, Bill Fisher says, led indirectly to changes and ructions. If such activities were to take place, it was felt HAPS should become a limited company. Now many more members had a say, among them one John Roast, who worked in the shipping industry and said he knew Barnes Wallis and various No 617 Squadron veterans well. At his instigation the Lancaster was

prepared to fly, the target being attendance at Scampton for a 'Dambusters' reunion in May 1967.

Preparing the aeroplane — not least painting it in RAF colours — was one thing. Getting the Air Registration Board's go-ahead was quite another. In both, the Field's engineers, led by Arthur Heath, were instrumental. As for a pilot, since there were then no other flying Lancasters, nobody was current on type. However, one supremely versatile man sprang to mind. Known to Fisher through the Tiger Club, Neil Williams was serving as a Royal Aircraft Establishment test pilot at Farnborough. Among other types, he flew large piston-engined taildraggers in the form of the Shackleton MR2 and Hastings.

"I was approached and asked if I would like to find a crew and carry out the flight testing", wrote Williams in the 1976 *Royal Air Force Yearbook*. "I had never flown a Lancaster, but as chance would have it, I had flown Lincolns for a short period. I started sounding out the flight engineers at Farnborough and was almost overwhelmed by their enthusiasm. Eventually the crew was selected; three very experienced flight engineers, all with previous Lancaster experience, and two of the most experienced navigators..."

On the morning of 6 May 1967, Williams took NX611 into the air. He was, as he wrote, "primarily interested in proving the functioning of all systems and in familiarising myself with the aircraft". Interestingly, he noted that the tropical radiators, a legacy of the machine's overseas service, caused him to cruise at a higher rpm so as to avoid engine temperatures dropping too low. "All things considered", he concluded, "the Lancaster was a big gentle docile aeroplane — or so we thought after that first uneventful flight. We had yet to see it show its teeth, and we didn't have very long to wait."

It happened the next day, when a second flight was conducted to, in Williams' words, "prove the feathering mechanism on all four engines, and to time undercarriage and flap retraction". Several supernumeraries were on board, including Ruhr Dams raid nose gunner Douglas Webb DFM. Perhaps it wasn't the most sensible idea to carry anything other than essential crew on such an early test flight, because a lot went wrong.

On feathering the port inner engine, "instead of stopping, it started to accelerate again, gradually at first, but then with alarming rapidity… I just had time to shout 'runaway prop' before all communication was swamped by an ear-splitting blare of sound that stunned the mind with an awesome ferocity. I pulled the nose up as quickly as I dared, to kill the airspeed, because that was the source of the terrible energy being absorbed by the propeller". Rapid intervention by pilot and engineer failed to slow the prop, so Williams resorted to desperate measures. "Even at reduced power on three engines the Lancaster was climbing fast as the speed fell, so I selected wheels and flaps down — I needed high drag, and quickly."

The Lancaster entered a cloud layer, whereupon Williams noticed that the horizon had toppled. Air speed dropped to 100kt, so he gradually lowered the nose. At least the three 'good' engines seemed to be running fine, while the overspeed had stabilised. But the radio and intercom had failed, and likewise the on-board fire extinguisher, which the engineer had engaged when the fire warning light lit up. With fire trucks on stand-by, ❯

TOP: By the time G-ASXX reached Biggin, the *Spirit of Surfers Paradise* name and artwork had been joined by a variety of sponsors' stickers and other 'zaps' picked up along the way. DENIS J. CALVERT

MIDDLE: Freshly repainted, but as yet without any squadron codes, NX611 is air-tested by the late Neil Williams. He enjoyed the type's handling. VIA LYNN WILLIAMS

ABOVE: The early throes of a privately owned UK warbird scene, to use a phrase never heard then: at September 1967's Blackbushe display, the Lancaster appeared on the same bill as Charles Masefield's P-51D Mustang. Neither would linger long on the circuit, alas. Behind are rows of Westland Dragonfly helicopters stored at the Surrey aerodrome. PETER BROWN

ABOVE:
Leaving Biggin for Filton's June 1968 display, the last it undertook at a public event. BRIAN GOULDING

Finally, the engineer came up on the intercom from the centre fuselage. The plan was that they would empty the contents of their tins into the reservoir and on the word of command I would select gear down. There was much grunting and swearing, accompanied by the rattling of empty cans rolling down the fuselage, following which I selected 'down'. All of this resulted in one red light for the port leg, which was obviously optimistic since I was looking at the port nacelle, and I had never seen anything so firmly shut in my life.

"We knew that there was only one possibility left — there is a compressed air system which should blast the gear down regardless of the position of the undercart lever; the only question was, would it operate correctly? If only one leg came down we would be worse off than ever. We discussed the situation as we circled the airfield; if we had to use the foam strip at Manston who was going to foot the bill? We decided to try the compressed air. The engineer cut the wire and pulled the handle. There was a hiss, a couple of very satisfying thuds, and two green lights stared back at me! We even had enough air to get the flaps down."

A blown hydraulic pipe was the culprit, and rapidly resolved. Hawker Siddeley engineers checked all was well, and on completion of an uneventful fourth test flight, the aircraft — newly christened *Guy Gibson* by the former 617 CO's father — was awarded its permit to fly. It made the Scampton reunion on

a safe emergency landing was completed back at Biggin. Williams recorded the cause as a build-up of sludge in the propeller's constant-speed unit.

"There was a slight air of reluctance as we clambered aboard for the third time", he wrote. This was two days later, 9 May, inspections and ground-running having confirmed that the Merlins had virtually escaped damage. Williams' intuition was to be proved right. "The undercarriage had just locked up and I was staring suspiciously at the port inner when it suddenly started to spray hydraulic fluid. This was instantly confirmed by the engineer who had selected flaps up with no result. We selected flaps to neutral and checked the

hydraulic content, which proved conspicuous by its almost complete absence. The engineer then went aft and rummaged in the locker,

> **66** *If only one leg came down we would be worse off than ever* **99**

where we fortuitously kept a supply of hydraulic fluid in tins — we were learning!

"Meanwhile, I had the cockpit to myself as I circled the field.

RIGHT:
A typical 'beat-up' on arrival at Lavenham on the penultimate day of March 1969. As can just be seen, the aircraft had by now been christened *Guy Gibson*, with the *Spirit of Surfers Paradise* artwork retained in front of his name.
EAST ANGLIAN DAILY TIMES

19-20 May, Williams giving spirited displays on both days. He followed up with similarly memorable performances at Blackbushe that September, and Filton in June 1968. A volunteer group had managed to get a four-engined heavy bomber onto the airshow circuit. HAPS' feat was almost beyond belief.

But, within the organisation, all was not well. "Sadly", says Richard Taylor, then one of the younger members, "Filton was to be the last public display appearance she actually made. Sponsorship started to dry up and, again, she was effectively grounded. Some discontented members and a number of active directors began to seriously question the future for '611. John Roast was the catalyst for that. He had become one of the directors, and unfortunately he got on the wrong side of all the other directors because, without seeking permission, he offered the Lancaster's propellers to be used on Spitfires and suchlike in the *Battle of Britain* film, at a cost". Roast had an involvement with the production, being credited as an art department researcher. While the deal didn't happen, Taylor recalls, "It wasn't too well-received. It soon became clear there was a split amongst the group."

The upshot was that Roast persuaded attendees of an extraordinary general meeting in London during October 1968 that HAPS's assets should pass to a new company, Reflectaire, of which he and his wife would be directors. It was at this point that Bill Fisher and others ceased their involvement, while the switch to ownership by a private company led Jock Maitland to begin charging a parking fee for the Lancaster.

"We had no means of paying that sort of money", says Taylor, "and no income coming in". Searching for a new home, "we went to places like Thruxton, Blackbushe and Fairoaks, seeking to find out whether any of the airfield owners would be likely to want us and to allow public access. There was a lukewarm interest, but nothing came of it, so we started spreading our wings and going all over the place. It wasn't until we stumbled across the former USAAF base at Alpheton near Lavenham in Suffolk, which had been home to the 487th Bombardment Group in the war, that things started getting hopeful. We made every effort to see David Alston, who was the farmer and owned most of that land. We

had a good session with him, and, to put it in short, he agreed."

As some of the volunteers began preparing the Lavenham control tower as the group's headquarters, so two experienced ex-Lancaster technicians now working for Hawker Siddeley readied NX611. The first of the ex-HAPS, now Reflectaire airframes to arrive was static Canadair Sabre Mk4 G-ATBF, roaded in from Biggin by mid-February 1969. The 'Lanc' should soon have followed, but the ailerons needed re-covering, a job carried out at Woodford, and the engines testing after such a long period of inactivity. With another permit to fly issued at the eleventh hour, Neil Williams took off for Lavenham on 30 March, NX611's journey being filmed for the BBC, while Richard Taylor was on board to shoot cine film. On arrival, another of Neil's trademark displays ensued. Nobody else, those who witnessed them would concur, has ever demonstrated a 'Lanc' like him.

---------------------- ❖ ----------------------

The move seemed to bring new impetus. "We were starting to get well-known as an attraction", recalls Richard Taylor. He had been taken on as a full-time Reflectaire employee, joining John Roast and another long-standing member, Martin Collins. Regular Lancaster engine runs were staged, Gp Capt Leonard Cheshire visiting on one unforgettable occasion in April with his wife Sue Ryder and their two children. Roast asked if Cheshire would like to perform the run himself, an invitation the former 617 'boss' accepted with alacrity. Then

came the suggestion that he might wish to taxi NX611 a short distance. As it set off, the 'Lanc' crushed one of its wheel chocks, mistakenly left in place. Heading along the perimeter track, about to take a left-hand bend, the turn suddenly tightened and NX611 ended up with its port mainwheel stuck in a ploughed field. No damage was done, and a profusely apologetic Cheshire signed the aircraft's logbook, "All 4 engines run, all functioning OK — Edge of runway soft."

The Reflectaire Preservation Group collection was enlarged, the ex-HAPS Seafire FR47 VP441 finally being brought in from Culdrose that July, and various military vehicles added. Yet the set-up was just too hand-to-mouth. "Towards the autumn", says Taylor, "it was getting a little bit awkward as far as negotiations with the farmer for a proper lease on the airfield site were concerned. It came to a situation when he made it clear that we were not paying rent we should have been paying. He was insistent that unless it were paid very soon, we would have to get off the airfield. It was unfortunate, because we thought we'd built up quite a good relationship, but again it was a funding issue, the same as it was at Biggin Hill to a degree. We just weren't getting the footfall we needed to keep things on the straight and narrow.

"There were occasions when both Martin and I had to go to our parents to see whether they would be able to put any money forward as a loan, to help us out of a ➲

LEFT:
Leonard Cheshire, Sue Ryder and family about to embark on an eventful taxi run.
MARTIN COLLINS

ABOVE: By 21 July 1969, the 'Lanc' had been coded GL-C in honour of Leonard Cheshire, whose first name was actually Geoffrey. Being reassembled in the foreground after delivery from Culdrose to Lavenham is Seafire FR47 VP441, much later restored to airworthiness by Ezell Aviation of Breckenridge, Texas, for owner James Smith. Not currently flown, VP441 resides on loan at the Stonehenge Air Museum near Fortine, Montana.
RICHARD TAYLOR

situation temporarily. Both parents did. When we first joined as full-time employees we were promised £20 a week... but we said that, until Reflectaire got on its feet, we'd use our own personal savings from our previous jobs, just to keep things ticking over. Of course, we hadn't received a penny by the time that winter occurred."

With a deadline to leave of 31 December, time was running out. Reflectaire was in no position to argue with the farmer, so it had to repeat the process of making the 'Lanc' airworthy and finding somewhere to ferry it to. "Again", says Richard, "we ended up at John Roast's home down in Surrey, sitting there night after night worrying about where we could go. We went out on the search, looking at places like Silverstone. They welcomed us to the site, and it would have been quite easy for the 'Lanc' to touch down there, but whether we would have been able to operate there as a functioning, flying aircraft after we got in was debatable... Unfortunately, it didn't suit what our intentions would be."

Some strings having been pulled, the Ministry of Defence put out an all-stations notice, asking every RAF station commander if they could assist. A tentative offer of Hemswell, a wartime Bomber Command base, looked perfect, but was soon withdrawn as the site was earmarked for disposal. Dishforth, Kemble and South Cerney were all felt unsuitable. "In the end", Taylor

remembers, we suddenly got a letter saying we had been offered a hangar at Hullavington... Of course we jumped at it and shot over there to view the place. We got a cold reception, basically because I don't think it turned out that the CO was too eager for us to be there. I think some pressure may have been applied behind the scenes — I can't be too sure — and in the end it was agreed that we should fly in there."

The Hawker Siddeley engineers did their inspections, good friends

---

> ## 66 *We spent night after night worrying about where we could go* 99

---

at RAF Wattisham provided fuel, Castrol donated 96 gallons of oil and Smiths Industries gave Reflectaire a complete set of new spark plugs. On 30 December, Taylor and Collins headed over to Lavenham. "Martin and I battled the winter weather to get all the spark plugs replaced, in the open. It didn't help that, two days before that, we had a snowfall. But we managed to get it done with the help of Brian Arbery, who was one of the active Reflectaire members."

Neil Williams' piloting services were secured, and departure set for

7 February. Once more John Roast drummed up publicity, the BBC's *Nationwide* programme covering the flight. As a result of that it was arranged for *Dam Busters* actor Richard Todd to be on board, along with former No 617 Squadron gunners Douglas Webb and Gerry Witherick. Waiting for NX611's arrival at Hullavington were several Operation 'Chastise' veterans and, in a rare public appearance, Guy Gibson's widow Eve. Another low-level display ensued, passing over the hangar in which the 'Lanc' was to be housed. "Everything went well on the day", says Richard Taylor, "and we thought this could be a new beginning. Unfortunately it didn't turn out that way."

Just 11 days later, Reflectaire received a letter from the MoD. The Hullavington station commander had directed, in Taylor's words, "that under no circumstances were we to advertise our presence on the airfield to the public and no members of the public would be allowed to visit". Any ideas of establishing a museum were killed stone-dead. The objective now became to "get as much done as we could while we were under cover, knowing that at some stage or another we would have to make another move."

A Hawker Siddeley engineer carried out an airframe inspection, while the engines were checked according to a schedule provided by Rolls-Royce. "We had a problem with the number three Merlin", says Taylor. "When we took the head off, we found that one of the retaining bolts had completely split". Had it flown in this condition, the camshaft could have failed completely. The equipment on hand didn't allow the cylinder head unit to be removed on its own, so eventually the entire block was taken off for transportation to Portsmouth-based A. H. Hawes and Sons, who sourced and fitted a new head. Back on NX611 by mid-May, the unit ran well again. A Rolls-Royce engineer was satisfied with all four powerplants; likewise an eight-strong Hawker Siddeley team with the airframe. The Lancaster was ready to go.

So was Neil Williams, though that had been a close-run thing. On 3 June, Neil was practising overhead Hullavington for the impending World Aerobatic Championships in Zlín 526A G-AWAR when he pulled off a famous escape. The Reflectaire crew looked on during their lunch

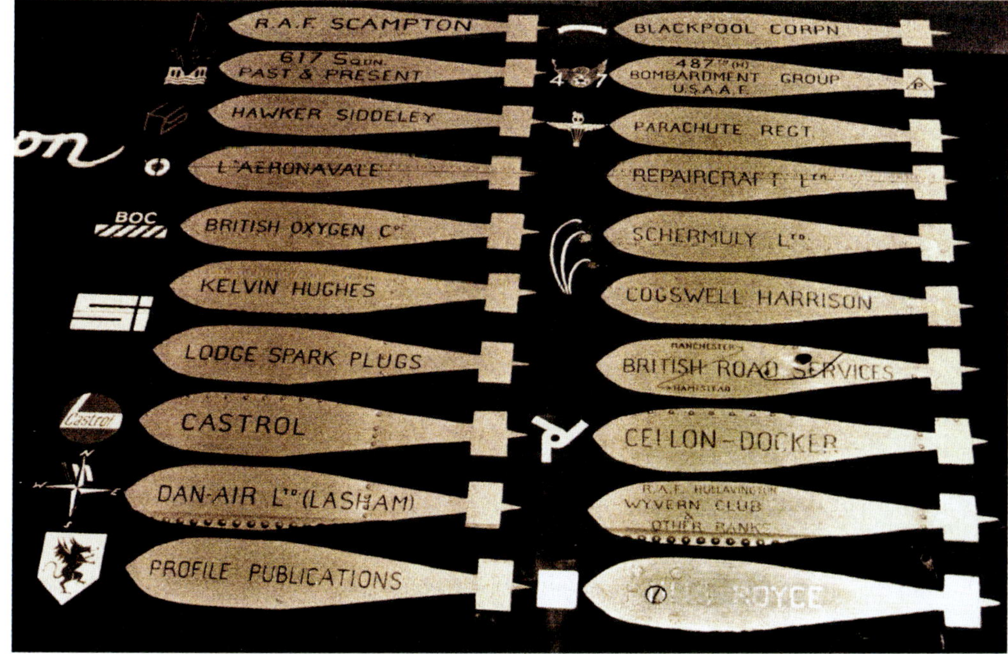

break, says Richard Taylor, "with our hearts in our throats" as the Zlín descended to very low level, inverted. Little did they know its port wing had folded up due to a fatigue failure, causing Williams to invert the aeroplane as a means of putting the wing back into a normal position before rolling erect just prior to touchdown. "He was so nonplussed when he was standing there next to the aircraft afterwards that it surprised everybody", recalls Taylor. "If he hadn't survived, goodness knows what we'd have done."

❖

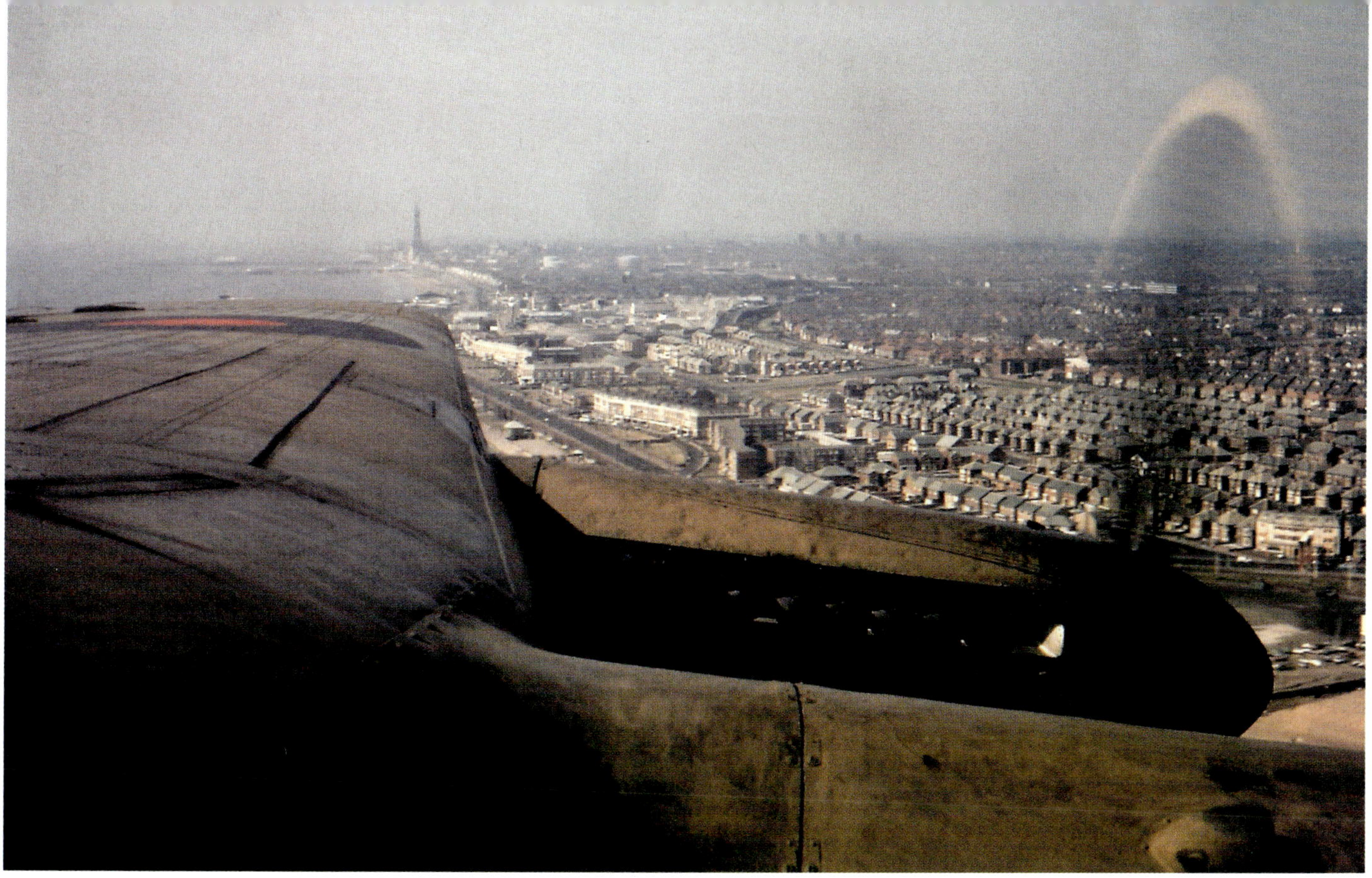

Through that supreme piece of instinctive airmanship, Williams was on hand to make what turned out to be NX611's final flight of the HAPS/Reflectaire era, just as he had been for all its others since the arrival at Biggin. The date was 26 June 1970, the destination Blackpool's Squires Gate airport. According to Richard, "When we were discussing it, knowing we had to move, we were sitting there saying the biggest problem we'd had was the fact we hadn't had the footfall — we hadn't had the freedom to allow the public access. Where could we possibly go? What type of venue would suit for us to establish ourselves? I'd been up to Blackpool years before, and I said it was a place that met the footfall requirement. With the number of people who visited Blackpool every year, I couldn't see how we'd fail."

With the airport management reasonably keen, agreement was forthcoming. The ferry flight included a very low-altitude diversion over Gwynedd's Bala Lake, much to the delight of ex-617 bomb-aimer Ron Valentine in his old position up front. After an hour-and-a-quarter, it was over, Williams setting NX611 onto the tarmac and taxiing up to a group of waiting onlookers, several Lancaster veterans residing in the area included. "Fourteen flights since she first arrived in '65 — I think we did pretty well as an amateur group, if you like", reflects Taylor.

They had, an impressive feat on a very tight budget. With the Lancaster, Seafire, Sabre and other exhibits, the outdoor 'museum' did bring visitors in during the summer. Yet still neither Taylor nor Collins had been paid, and there was only so much more unremunerated toil they were prepared to take. Both departed in the autumn of 1970, having expressed concerns about a lack of security for the museum compound and unfettered access to the 'Lanc' in particular. What was more, certain other attempts to drum up local support ended up costing more than they achieved.

A few new volunteers, not to mention the tireless help of ➔

ABOVE:
The last flight — for now — and an on-board view of finals to Blackpool, tower in background. BRIAN GOULDING

BELOW:
These 'credit bomb' symbols were applied to NX611's nose, thanking companies and organisations deemed instrumental in getting and keeping the aircraft flying. MARTIN COLLINS

RIGHT:
Neil Williams was at the controls of NX611 for all **14** occasions on which it took to the air following the delivery flight to Britain — whoever pilots it when next it flies has some big shoes to fill. Williams is second from right here, as the crew and some of the welcoming party walk away from the 'Lanc' at Blackpool. Next to him at far right is navigator Flt Lt Eric Hughes, who accompanied Neil every time.
WEST LANCASHIRE EVENING GAZETTE

BELOW:
Richard Todd about to board for the ferry flight from Lavenham to Hullavington.
RAY WOOD

BELOW RIGHT:
Guy Gibson's widow Eve was a centre of attention as NX611 arrived at Hullavington. Greeting her is No 617 Squadron Dams raid veteran Douglas Webb, who flew in the aeroplane several times, while Reflectaire boss John Roast looks on, cigarette in mouth.
MARTIN COLLINS

Air Training Corps and Girls' Venture Corps cadets, kept things running through 1971. Granada TV's use of NX611 in an episode of drama series *A Family at War*, for which 617 veteran Mark Flatman performed a taxi run, boosted the coffers a little. Alas, none of it was enough. Two things now happened at once. Blackpool council, owner of the airport, was owed substantial sums in rent and pursued the matter through the courts. On 5 November, it gave Reflectaire formal notice to leave. In London, the company was served a winding-up petition relating to unpaid wages. It went into voluntary liquidation, a court order requiring all assets to be sold by auction.

The result of the Blackpool sale, on 29 April 1972, is well-known — how the highest bid put in for the Lancaster was just £9,500, far lower

> ❝ *A court order required all Reflectaire's assets to be auctioned* ❞

than the £20,000 reserve price, after which Lord Lilford secured the purchase for £12,500 a couple of days later. HAPS and Reflectaire

may not have survived, but, thanks to them, NX611 had. This was the great accomplishment of the impecunious preservationists who saw the potential and pursued what some would have considered an impossible dream as far as they could go.

Richard Taylor surely speaks for many. "It was an experience in our lives we could never hope to regain. The positive side of it outweighed all the troubles we had. We wouldn't have missed it for the world — the tribulations as well..." **A**

With thanks to Lynn Williams, and credit to the book *The Story of a Lanc* (Version 5) by Brian Goulding and Richard J. A. Taylor.

TURN IT UP TO ONE-ELEVEN

Re-engining the BAC One-Eleven with Rolls-Royce Tay engines could have given the veteran British airliner a new lease of life — but neither BAe, nor the market, turned out to think so **WORDS:** BEN DUNNELL

British-built aircraft, converted in the USA, encouraged by the Saudis, with a view to production in Romania. It wasn't the most obvious partnership. Nor, as it transpired, was it one exactly made in heaven. But, for a while, it seemed to offer the best hope of giving an ageing design a fresh dose of relevance.

The subject was the BAC One-Eleven, which, as it approached its quarter-century, may have been considered increasingly 'old hat', but still flew with many airlines, corporate operators and others. Yet it faced one problem above all — its engines. The Rolls-Royce Spey was noisy and thirsty. Even hush-kitted versions would not meet the International Civil Aviation Organization's Chapter 3 noise requirements, and their Stage 3 equivalents from the US Federal Aviation Administration. Wayne Fagan, then senior vice president of commercial contracts and general counsel for The Dee Howard Co, recalls one memory of being with the firm's eponymous founder: "Dee and I were at the Paris Air Show, on the ramp near the chalets, and we heard this tremendous roar. I said, 'That's either got to be a BAC One-Eleven or a Mirage'. In fact, I think it was a Mirage…"

With new ICAO emissions regulations also in the offing, the timing of Romania's deal to licence-build Spey-powered One-Elevens could scarcely have been worse. Signed in 1978, as part of President Nicolae Ceausescu's desire to boost the country's aviation industry — and, in so doing, earn hard Western currency — it covered the manufacturing of Series 500 models, to be known as the ROMBAC One-Eleven, and their engines. Of

> ## " *The Tay seemed the answer to the One-Eleven's prayers* "

those, the first made its maiden flight on 18 September 1982. With the twin Speys, this was an aircraft out of time. Recognising this, the Romanians planned to stop turning out Spey-engined examples after the 12th to come off the Bucharest line.

Still, there was an almost ready-made solution. Rolls-Royce came up with what it initially dubbed the Hi-flow Spey, a high-bypass ratio development of the Spey Mk555-15. To indicate the extent of the changes, when officially launched in January 1983 it was known as the Tay Mk610-8, offering 12,420lb of thrust on take-off. It had been chosen for the new Gulfstream IV executive jet, and would soon be selected to power the Fokker 100, a much-altered successor to the F28 Fellowship. Quieter, cleaner, more efficient and easier to maintain, the Tay seemed the answer to the One-Eleven's prayers.

The team at British Aerospace's Weybridge facility, responsible for the One-Eleven, certainly thought so. During 1983 they actively promoted a re-engining effort, albeit without attracting any orders. And, as we shall see, there was internal opposition. If any such programme were to go ahead, a new partner would clearly have to be found.

Enter — via a roundabout route The Dee Howard Co, based in San Antonio, Texas. As Wayne Fagan describes, "It really started with the thrust reverser that Dee helped to bring to market that had been designed and patented by a French engineer, Etienne Fage, called the Howard-Fage Cold Flow Thrust Reverser. It was for the new high-bypass jet engines. I think the first aircraft we put that on was the BAe 125-800, and the second was the Dassault Falcon 20. Anyhow, it was a terrific product.

"Always thinking, Dee realised he had this great reverser, and he was interested in getting into the nacelle business, so as to sell the reverser ❯

TOP:
Installation of the Tay 650s and associated thrust reversers taking place. The engine was heavier and more powerful than the Spey it replaced, requiring a certain amount of strengthening, and the use of beefed-up pylons. VIA WAYNE FAGAN

ABOVE:
By this stage, the Dee Howard-designed cowlings have been fitted.
VIA WAYNE FAGAN

and the nacelle together. But he felt there were established companies out there in the nacelle business, and it would be very difficult for The Dee Howard Co to break into it. He was looking for a re-engining programme where he could use the nacelle on a re-engined aircraft, and then expand from there."

Serendipitously, Fagan continues, "We had Saudi customers that had BAC One-Elevens". One of the Saudi Series 400s was owned by Sheikh Salem bin Laden, the oldest Bin Laden son and the then head of the Bin Laden Group. Salem also owned a Learjet which had Dee Howard

products on it, and he served as an unofficial advisor to the Saudi royal family on a head of state Boeing 747-300 Dee Howard was completing at the same time. This was just the sort of high-level backing the Tay One-Eleven needed, even if the Tay 612-14 — equivalent to the Fokker 100's Tay 620-15 — was, in Fagan's words, "a little lower-thrust than we were interested in."

Negotiations went on through 1985 and '86, revealing all sorts of unforeseen complexities. "Dee went to England and visited with British Aerospace and Rolls", recalls Wayne Fagan. "He [...] said he would like

BAe to make available to us the baseline data for the BAC One-Eleven, because with the FAA — and probably the CAA as well — for any sort of retrofit you have to show that the modified aircraft is as good as or better than the unmodified one. To reproduce the baseline data would have been cost-prohibitive. That's when things got very complicated. It became highly political."

Partly key to this was the licensing deal the Romanians had finalised to build the ROMBAC One-Elevens and their engines. "BAe and Rolls insisted that, if we were to develop the product, we negotiate in good faith to make the technology available to the Romanians under terms and conditions to be agreed between Dee Howard and the Romanians. It became my job to conduct those good faith negotiations on behalf of Dee Howard with the Romanians.

"I spent four-and-a-half years on a circuit. I would go to London and meet with senior officials in BAe and Rolls; then I flew to Bucharest, to meet the Romanian company CNIAR [Centrul National al Industriei Aeronautice Române] and the British ambassador. I would come back to London to debrief Rolls, BAe and the head of the eastern European desk at the Department of Trade and Industry, and on occasion the chair of the [House of Commons] foreign affairs select committee.

"On one of these occasions I was meeting the very nice gentleman from the DTI in his office. I'll never forget it. He said to me, 'Wayne, how can Her Majesty's Government help you?' For a young lawyer from San Antonio, that was quite a shocker! Jokingly, I told him, 'Well, it's costing a lot in R&D. We could use money'. But I wondered why he had such an interest in this project. He explained that the loan to the Romanians to make available the money to pay the royalties to BAe and Rolls was loaned to the Romanian government by a consortium of five banks in London. The loan repayment was guaranteed by the British government. If the Romanian programme wasn't successful, they would default and the British government would have to pay.

"But more importantly, he said, 'Wayne, some day the Berlin Wall is going to come down. We don't know when that's going to happen, but it will happen at some point in time. We do not want the failure of the BAC One-Eleven programme in Romania to be a black mark against British industry in eastern Europe'. I thought, wow, that's real insight and forward thinking."

The official, public launch of the Dee Howard project took place in March 1986. Confirmation came several months later that it was to cover all variants of the One-Eleven, not just the Series 400 as first announced. Operators of the 475 and 500 models would be able to benefit too — good news for the ROMBAC programme, which had started out by building the 560 version. Conversion of a Tay-engined prototype was to involve an ex-American Airlines Series 401AK, latterly modified as an executive transport. In period reports, Dee Howard gave an expected first flight date of June 1987, with FAA type certification by the end of that year.

BAe was described as furnishing "technical assistance", a euphemistic phrase reflecting the reality of its interest in the Tay One-Eleven. Certain British attempts to drum up backing for Tay conversions had foundered in large part through the company's attitude. As Wayne Fagan puts it, "There were two political groups within BAe, shall I say. One was the group that developed the BAe 146 [at Hatfield], and the other was the BAC One-Eleven group out of Weybridge. The 146 [...] had not been doing well commercially. They saw the re-engined One-Eleven as a threat to the 146."

That said, the situation did reportedly improve, thanks to the Saudi connection. This, remember, was the formative period of the very controversial Al Yamamah arms deal between the UK and Saudi Arabia, the first stage of which brought an order in September 1985 for military equipment including 72 Tornados and 30 Hawks. According to Fagan, "In a meeting between

> ## 66 *They saw the re-engined One-Eleven as a threat to the BAe 146* 99

senior Saudi officials and the British government, Rolls and BAe — I wasn't there, but I heard this — with regard to the Tornados, the Saudis said, 'By the way, how's the One-Eleven programme going?' I think a message was sent and things became a little easier after that."

Not so easy, though, as to prevent the schedule slipping. Before long, Dee Howard was talking about flying the prototype more than a year after its previous estimate, with a two-year delay to certification. Substituting the Tay 612 for the more powerful Tay 650 alleviated performance concerns, while the 1987 Paris Air Show brought news that Sheikh Salem bin Laden was investing in the Dee Howard programme. Outwardly, prospects still appeared favourable. Then several unfortunate things happened in tandem.

"During this period of time", says Wayne Fagan, "there was an accident [on 26 April 1988] with an Aloha Airlines Boeing 737 in Hawaii where the top of the fuselage came off in flight. The crew showed incredible airmanship skills in landing that aircraft. But the issue of ageing aircraft became a big deal... It also left a question mark in the eyes of the industry. That put us in a serious bind about cashflow". Just weeks later, on 29 May, Salem bin Laden died in the crash of his Sprint ultralight aircraft in San Antonio.

"By 1988 we should have had the aircraft in production, but because of all these delays we didn't", Fagan continues. "While we were encountering delays in the certification of the BAC One-Eleven, other phases of the business were going very well and Dee was beginning to think about succession planning and sustainability of The Dee Howard Co, so we began to have discussions with potential partners". Several suitors were approached, among them Tony Ryan, then the boss of the GPA ❯

LEFT:
BAe test pilot John Lewis conducts the much-delayed first flight on 2 July 1990, as viewed from the Learjet chase aircraft. VIA WAYNE FAGAN

Group, a leading airliner lessor and financier, and co-founder of Ryanair. GPA had seen potential in the Tay One-Eleven — specifically, new production in Bucharest — and there had earlier been an effort to bring it into the programme.

While discussions were ongoing between Dee and Tony Ryan, and between Dee and a London-based investment group, a new potential partner entered the discussions: Aeritalia. "We hadn't had any contact with Aeritalia", Wayne continues, "but they had very close ties with UPS through doing maintenance work for them. Aeritalia also had relations with Rolls-Royce. Apparently, UPS had told Aeritalia they needed to have a US base of operations or they couldn't continue to do business. They started scrambling, heard about Dee Howard and contacted us. Dee and I went over to Rome for an introductory meeting, just to start a dialogue, and wound up walking out with a deal."

That day in the spring of 1988 saw Aeritalia buying a 40 per cent stake in Dee Howard, increased a few months down the line to 60 per cent. Still, though, there was a paucity of actual movement. A long list of potential customers saw only minor progress; Wayne Fagan remembers positive talks with Peter Villa of British Island Airways, while Dan-Air and GPA were also in the market, amongst many others. Furthermore, Ken Goddard wrote in his definitive history, *The Rolls-Royce Tay Engine and the BAC One-Eleven* (Rolls-Royce Heritage Trust, 2000), "Rolls-Royce started to send invoices for overdue payments."

With British firm Swift Aviation/Associated Aerospace launching its own programme, seeking to involve new Romanian-manufactured machines, the overall impression at this stage is one of confusion. The degree of management upheaval within Dee Howard rather bears this out. Wayne Fagan returned to his private law practice, although — like Howard himself — he stayed on the board of directors of The Dee Howard Co until Aeritalia completed its takeover.

Interested parties ebbed away, GPA deciding against the Tay One-Eleven, while British Island Airways found itself in mounting financial difficulties. There was insufficient market support to sustain one re-engining programme, let alone multiple offerings. And in the

background of any proposals, like that from Swift/Associated, involving Romanian production was the fact that just nine Spey-engined ROMBAC aircraft had been built since 1982, of which seven had been delivered. Would there be a miraculous upswing of output?

> **❝ Just a few customers were still at the table, each with small fleets ❞**

The maiden flight of Dee Howard's Tay One-Eleven prototype provided some cause for celebration. It took place in San Antonio on 2 July 1990, BAe test pilot — and Shuttleworth Collection pilot — John Lewis at the controls, accompanied by Ron Franzen from the American company.

The one-and-three-quarter-hour sortie passed off largely without a hitch, this despite how Goddard records that the aeroplane itself, re-registered N650DH, had been the subject of adverse comment from Rolls-Royce representatives regarding its maintenance state. The tailplane, for instance, had to be replaced in its entirety.

Given the circumstances, flying the aircraft trans-Atlantic for appearances in the UK might have been felt a step too far, not least considering how behind schedule the test-flying was. However, N650DH did make the trip, generating some good publicity when flights from Birmingham Airport in late August showed just how much quieter the Tay-engined machine — dubbed the Series 2400 — was compared to the Spey-powered original. It followed that up with daily displays at the Farnborough show. Literature distributed there by Dee Howard cited a 17 per cent reduction in fuel burn, a 20 per cent increase in range, and a 32 per cent time-to-climb reduction. These figures were never fully verified in flight.

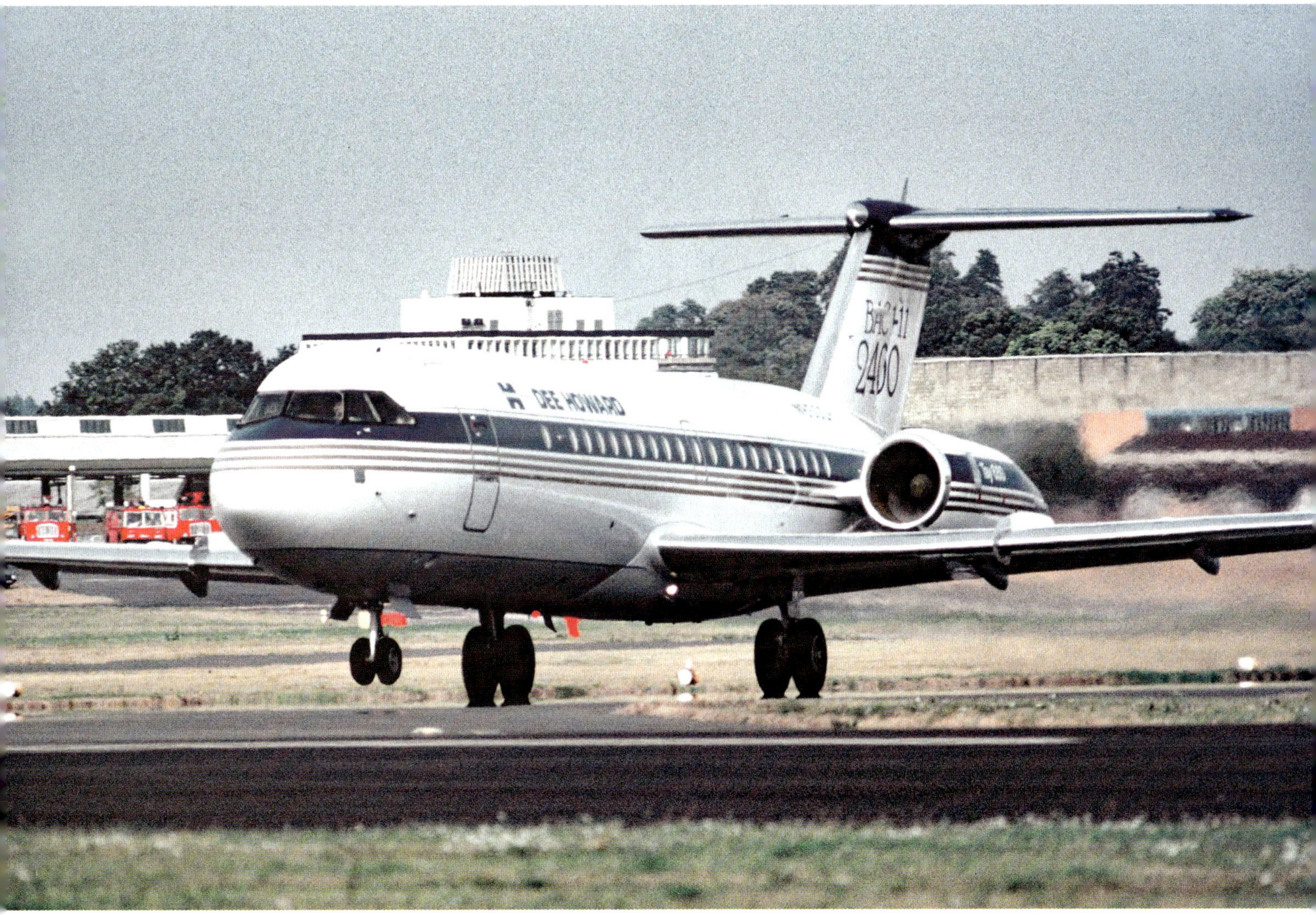

Renewed sales pitches mounted as 1990 drew to a close seemed to confirm the inevitable. Just a few customers were still at the table, each of them with One-Eleven fleets that could be counted on the fingers of a single hand. Worse, perhaps, flight trials had not run wholly smoothly. Goddard wrote that use of full reverse thrust shook the tailplane so badly it exceeded the maximum loads, while N650DH failed water ingestion tests on a wet runway.

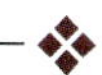

Certification turned into a merry-go-round, the FAA approaching the process as if the One-Eleven 2400 was all-new, rather than a variant of an existing design. Dee Howard secured another Series 400, N333GB from HM Industries, which became the second converted aircraft — the firm's hope was to take some of the burden away from N650DH and speed things up. It duly flew in July 1991, conducting avionics test-flying out of Phoenix, Arizona. This proved successful, but far from enough to save the programme's bacon.

Alenia, as Aeritalia was now called, had a decision to make. Retrospectively, with certification stalled, it probably wasn't all that difficult. The Italian company blamed BAe for issues relating to structural analysis data, the main stumbling-block. Both test aircraft were grounded in mid-late November 1991, suspension of the project becoming public during December. Now the real wrangling started, Alenia suing BAe over the alleged non-supply of data. It was the first of four lawsuits, this one, Ken Goddard's book states, being resolved out of court. The Dee Howard programme was never publicly cancelled — indeed, there were efforts to restart both it and Romanian production — but, rather, fizzled out. The number of Bucharest-built airframes thus remained stuck at nine. The two Dee Howard test aircraft, meanwhile, were scrapped at San Antonio.

At this distance, without resorting to too much hindsight, it is difficult to assess the Tay One-Eleven's real prospects. Had the problems thrown up by flight trials been eradicated, there seems little doubt the aircraft/engine combination would have worked. Proof of the Tay's qualities comes from its long-running use in the Fokker 70/100 and Gulfstream IV families — and, indeed, the Boeing 727-100 freighters of UPS which were re-engined by Dee Howard. Would a timelier path to test-flying and certification have smoothed the way to orders? Perhaps, but it can only ever be speculation.

Had BAe been more supportive at an earlier stage, one can understand how the Tay conversion could have gained a foothold. However, it had its own understandable reasons for being reluctant. Maybe the easiest — or most simplistic — conclusion is that the Tay One-Eleven was destined to fail all along.

ABOVE: Farnborough 1990 turned out to be the Tay One-Eleven's only significant public showing.
DENIS J. CALVERT

Robs Lamplough's Bf 109 E-1 in the Meier Motors workshops at Bremgarten, Germany.
VIA PLATINUM FIGHTERS

EXCEPTIO

As a Spanish Civil War veteran, the Messerschmitt Bf 109 E-1 owned by Robs Lamplough is among the most significant warbird restorations of recent times. But, as a new custodian is sought, what's the history of this very special fighter?

WORDS: BEN DUNNELL

n every way, it's exceptional. A veritable 'time capsule' of a German fighter, its Spanish Civil War combat history with the Legion Condor well-documented, in the hands of the same owner for more than 40 years and the subject of an outstanding restoration. Only now is it being offered for sale, whereupon a new custodian will take on a unique piece of aviation history, and hopefully see it through to flying condition.

For decades, the Messerschmitt Bf 109 E-1 coded 6-88 was out of the limelight, but never forgotten. Robs Lamplough, one of the true pioneers of the UK's warbird scene, was waiting for the right time to move the project forward. That

process started in 2012, when it was moved from storage in Britain to the Meier Motors workshops at Bremgarten, southern Germany. The result will be the oldest airworthy Bf 109 in the world. But what makes this aeroplane so special?

For Robs, its recovery came about through a friend. "I knew a Swiss guy called Jan Lütjens [whose mother was Austrian]. His parents lived in Madrid, and his father worked for BMW, promoting the marque in the whole of Spain. They were a lovely family, and I knew them very well. He told me enthusiastically about an auction sale coming up with a lot of interesting aeroplanes. One of

CLOCKWISE FROM TOP LEFT: The Daimler-Benz DB601 engine of another J/88 Bf 109 frames 6-88. The number 6 was the type code for the Messerschmitt fighter with the Legion Condor. VIA PLATINUM FIGHTERS

The 'Emil' soon after its arrival with the Legion Condor, assigned to the 1. Staffel of Jagdgruppe 88 as the regular mount of the squadron's commanding officer, Hptm Siebelt Reents. VIA PLATINUM FIGHTERS

La Sénia, in the Tarragona province of Catalonia, was the home base for 1.J/88 and its Bf 109s, of which 6-88 was one of the first two E-1 models delivered. VIA PLATINUM FIGHTERS

While the second aircraft in this line of Bf 109s sports the 'Holzauge' (wooden eye) emblem of 1.J/88 — and, it seems, the third as well — 6-88 remains rather anonymous in its markings. VIA PLATINUM FIGHTERS

NAL 'EMIL'

them was a Heinkel He 111 H-16, with a German-built airframe, and another was a Bf 109, also German-built. There was no engine in the 109, but other than that it was very complete."

Even then, in 1981, it was remarkable that the 'Emil' had survived in derelict condition for so long without a keen collector snapping it up. Sixteen years earlier, accounts have it that Spanish aviation journalist Luis Ignacio Azaola Reyes spotted the remains abandoned at León airfield, north-western Spain. He photographed them in situ, but still nobody stepped in. That changed with the auction, and Robs Lamplough's intervention. He bought the Bf 109

there, and effected a recovery himself: "I put it on a racing car trailer and towed it home behind a 6.9-litre Mercedes sedan."

> **There was no engine, but other than that it was very complete**

Once an initial period on loan to the Tangmere Military Aviation Museum was complete, the fighter went into storage pending

restoration. No Werknummer was found on the fuselage; the port wing is of Messerschmitt manufacture, but the starboard wing was taken from an aeroplane produced by Leipzig-based Erla. Further research is now divulging different part numbers within the wings, which will help tell more of the story. However, still visible on the empennage was the serial number C.5-88, as worn in Spanish Air Force service after World War Two. Despite the lack of a fuselage Werknummer, this shows that the aircraft would have been 6-88 with the Legion Condor, the German unit which deployed to Spain to fight for Franco's Nationalist side both in the air and on the ground.

And that, in turn, places it firmly in the pantheon of significant survivors. The first two Bf 109 E-1s for the Legion Condor were 6-87 and this very aircraft, 6-88, built in Augsburg and delivered by sea to Spain in the summer of 1938. Entering service with the 1. Staffel of Jagdgruppe 88 (1.J/88), stationed at La Sénia, they augmented the Bf 109 C and D models already in the group's inventory. Starting with three prototypes in late 1936, J/88 pioneered the combat employment of the Messerschmitt fighter. The Staffelkapitän of its first squadron, 1.J/88, was Hptm Siebelt Reents, and during September 1938 he took on the brand-new 6-88 as his personal mount.

It is not known which Bf 109 Reents was flying on 6 February 1939, when he claimed the kill of a fighter belonging to the Spanish Republican air arm. His victim is sometimes described as "a Curtiss", though this seems unlikely, given that no Curtiss fighters are recorded as having served with the Republicans. Among later assignments, Reents went on to fly with II./JG 27 during the Battle of Britain, be posted to a night fighter group headquarters and take part in the North African campaign, ending the war flying Focke-Wulf Fw 190s in Denmark. He died in May 2012, aged 101. Several photos exist showing Reents with 6-88 in Spain.

By the time of his aerial kill, the civil war was approaching its end. J/88 flew its final sortie on 27 March 1939, escorting Heinkel He 111 bombers of Kampfgruppe 88 (K/88) on a strike against forward Republican positions. The Nationalist victory was inevitable, and a ceasefire was declared on 1 April. The Legion Condor's men, and most of its machines, returned home to Germany. However, a certain quantity of materiel remained in Spain, handed over to Franco's regime. A number of Bf 109 Es in-country when the civil war concluded were passed to the 'new' Spanish Air Force, the Ejército del Aire (EdA). Among them was 6-88, flown initially to

> ## 66 *New details have come to light since a Deutsches Museum expert was able to examine the 109 in depth* 99

León and subsequently to Logroño-Agroncillo, where it joined the strength of Grupo 25.

Now with the serial C.5-88, but still marked as 6-88, the Messerschmitt is known to have experienced a mishap on 24 August 1939. In the hands of Teniente José Vincente Muntadas, it ran out of fuel and had to make a forced landing at Larraga in the Navarra area of northern Spain. Not for the last time, it was repaired and returned to service. By this point, the aircraft had received 20mm MG FF cannon in its wings, indicating an upgrade to Bf 109 E-3 standard. Perhaps this came about

via the wing swap which is known to have taken place at some juncture.

Moving with Grupo 25 to Reus at the end of 1940, C.5-88 and its fellow Bf 109 Es soldiered on with the EdA in front-line service long after the 'Emil' was obsolete as far as the Luftwaffe was concerned. In fact, some lingered after the end of the Second World War, 6-88 included. Lightning struck again on 16 May 1950 when, for the second time, it force-landed out of fuel. At the controls was Capt Vinicio Gil de Gómez — a test pilot stationed at Logroño — who reportedly suffered minor injuries when he put the Bf 109 down near Teruel.

His incident may have precipitated an official request on 19 September 1950 to withdraw 6-88 from service. This took place the following month, the aircraft being stored at the León maintenance facility. However, this still wasn't the end. It is believed an EdA technical officer who had previously flown Bf 109s repaired 6-88 — the serial of which changed to C.4E-88 during December 1951 — and returned it to airworthy condition for his own use as what has been described as a personal 'runabout'. Thus the civil war veteran carried on taking to the skies until 1957-58. One of the first two 'Emils' delivered to Spain had become the country's last genuine flying Bf 109, quite a landmark in a country where the front-line use of the Messerschmitt fighter had been honed in combat.

As the Bf 109's close cousin, the Spanish-built, Rolls-Royce Merlin-powered Hispano HA-1112 Buchón variant, flew on in EdA service until October 1965, so 6-88 sat at León, seeing utilisation as an instructional airframe. When finally it came to be restored, that process has since revealed fresh secrets. New details of its background have come to light since, in 2017, an expert from the Deutsches Museum in Munich was able to examine the 'Emil' in depth on Robs Lamplough's behalf. Another ex-Legion Condor example, Bf 109 E-3 Werknummer 790, is part of the museum's collection and as such provided a useful benchmark. Built as an E-1, that machine is exhibited in Luftwaffe colours, but carried the codes 6-106 during the Spanish Civil War.

Key to this forensic investigation was the ability to obtain paint samples from the layers remaining on different areas of the airframe,

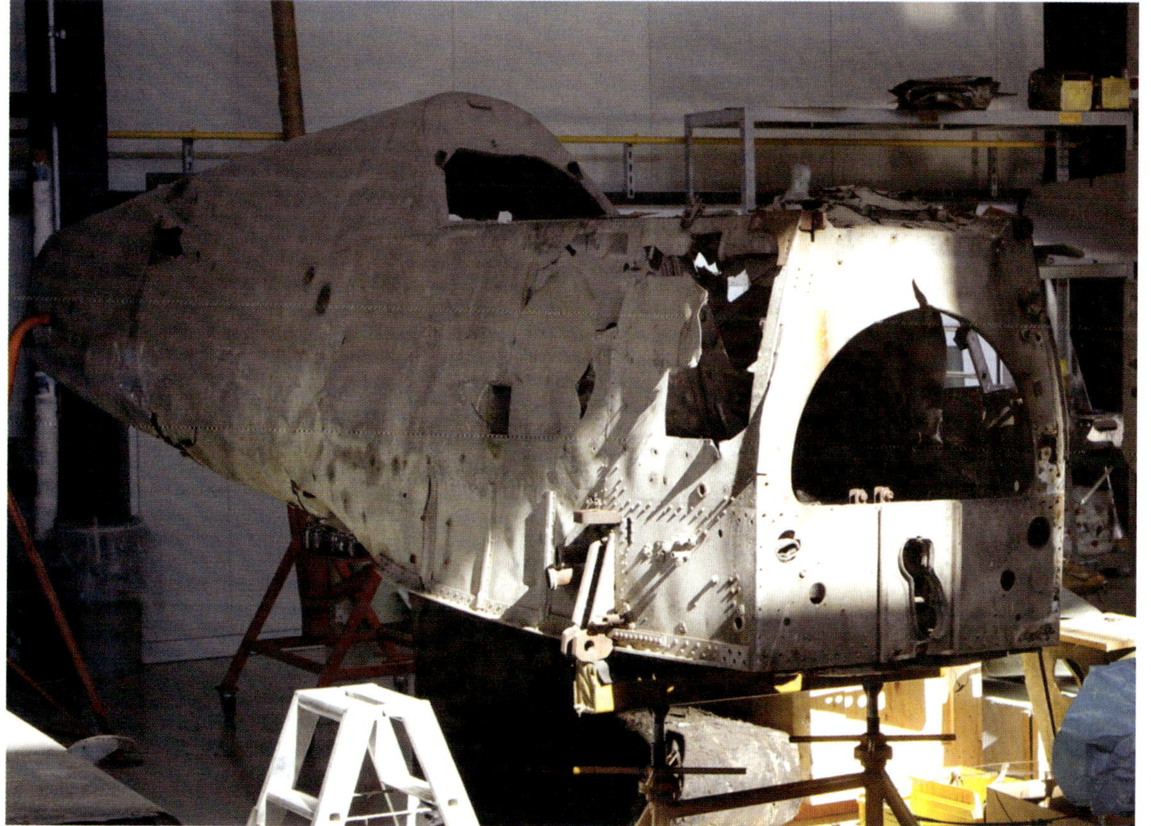

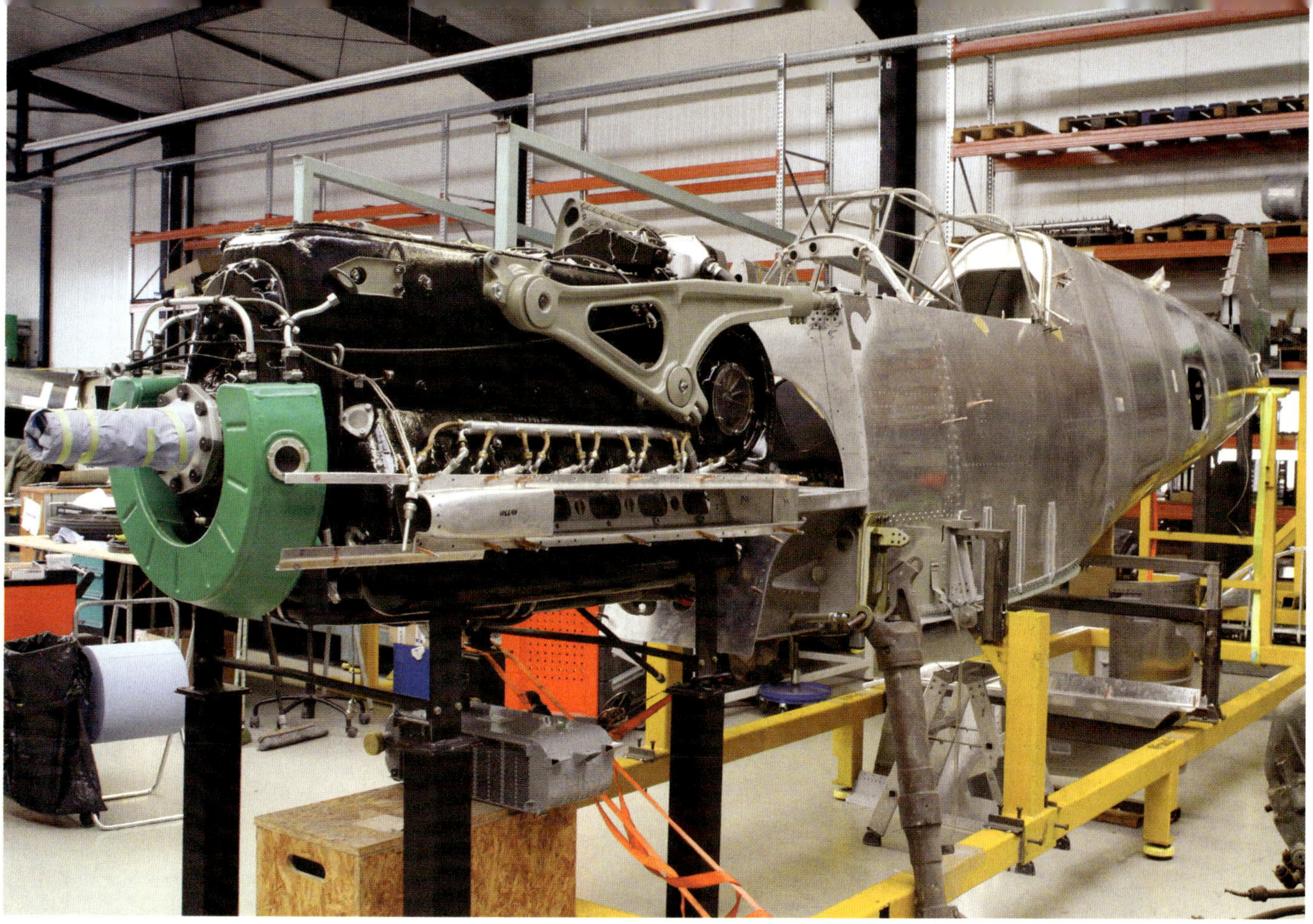

which could be compared using a spectrometer with samples taken from the original paint of 6-106 and parts known to come from two other Legion Condor 'Emils'. One was the wreck of 6-130, which crashed at El Prat del Llobregat airfield in Barcelona during a display in December 1940 and was excavated in the course of construction work on the third runway at what is now Barcelona Airport. It is preserved by the Centro de Aviación Histórica in La Sénia. The other was a cabin roof frame — probably from a Bf 109 B — in private ownership.

Only a few areas of 6-88's paint had been preserved after so long, mainly those dating from the aircraft's manufacture and its time with the Legion Condor. This was as a result of a small amount of fire damage and natural weathering by the elements, the rear fuselage

ABOVE: Come the spring of 2018, the fuselage had been rebuilt and the DB601 engine returned from Vintage V-12s and fitted. MATTHIAS DORST

LEFT: It has proved possible to reuse a good many original elements of the fuselage, which is pictured in the Meier Motors facility before dismantling began. MATTHIAS DORST

ABOVE:
Analysis of paint samples from this and the Deutsches Museum's Bf 109 E-3 has enabled the precise replication of the Legion Condor colours and markings on 6-88.
VIA ROBS LAMPLOUGH

and the wings having escaped best. One interesting find was evidence of a large numerical marking extending as far as the tail section. This indicates part of a three-digit code, most likely ending in a 4.

What all this has enabled is the application of a colour scheme as true as possible to that worn with 1.J/88 in 1938-39. When Meier Motors received the aircraft in 2012, it set about a restoration befitting the airframe's background. It was given an in-depth inspection, the original parts being catalogued. In creating repair jigs for the wings and fuselage, original Messerschmitt plans and procedures were followed throughout, after which the meticulous process of dismantling and rebuilding got under way. While the wings and fuselage have required new skins, a large quantity of original material has been retained in both cases. It was decided to restore the wings to Bf 109 E-1 configuration without the 20mm cannon fit.

The Daimler-Benz DB601A engine went to Vintage V-12s at Tehachapi, California, for overhaul, while Hertfordshire-based Skycraft has finished the VDM propeller. The latter was among the more recent items to be ticked off the list, together with the hydraulic

> **❝ A large amount of the original wing and fuselage material has been retained in the restoration ❞**

and electrical systems, and the engine cowlings. Once the cowlings were ready and fitted, the engine was temporarily removed to allow upgrade and modification work, which was still ongoing at the time of writing. The precaution has been taken to reserve a German registration, D-FCON.

The Bf 109 E is offered by Platinum Fighter Sales for sale on an 'as is, where is' basis. As Robs Lamplough (see *Aeroplane* September 2023) told the author recently, "I've got to the point where I can no longer fly it, and my enthusiasm will naturally wane. The cost of keeping it and the amount I've spent on it are totally disproportionate". Now the result of that considerable investment is ready to move on — and, most excitingly, to fly. In so doing, it will tell an historical story of immense importance. The Spanish Civil War was the cauldron in which the Luftwaffe refined its tactics and its aircraft, ready for the wider global conflict to come. No other airworthy aircraft represents that period, and the attention to detail with which 6-88 has been restored will bring it to life in the most meaningful fashion. **A**

Anyone with a serious interest in purchasing the Bf 109 should contact Platinum Fighter Sales via www.platinumfighters.com

TRIAL AND ERROR

The first edition of the Lympne light aeroplane trials took place 100 years ago — and didn't exactly swing a lamp over the future. How did the correspondents of the time view it?

WORDS: BEN DUNNELL

Women's emancipation was not a concept to which C. G. Grey devoted a great deal of thought. The many feats of female aviators during his tenure as editor of *The Aeroplane* often drew short shrift, if not downright bigotry. Even in the wake of the first Lympne light aeroplane trials — officially described as competitions for 'motorgliders', a rather different sense of that term than we know today — he could not resist putting into print an unnecessary slight.

"There are sundry optimists in the Trade", he wrote in the 17 October 1923 edition, "who think that these Competitions open up a new era in Civil Aviation. They believe that there is a market for motorgliders if they can be put on the market at a reasonable price — say £200 or thereabouts. On this point one entirely disagrees, for the optimists entirely disregard the fact that for practical purposes there is no market for a single-seater motor vehicle of any kind. And this is due to the psychological fact that as soon as

a mere male has enough money to buy and maintain a motor vehicle he promptly becomes an object of interest to some designing female.

"A number of single-seater motor-bicycles are sold, but how many continue to be single-seater? In a very short while the owner is compelled to attach a side-car, or if he cannot afford one he fits that species of pillion arrangement which is vulgarly known as a 'flapper-bracket'. Single-seater run-about cars have been put on the market, but invariably after a little time a woman

One of the star performers at Lympne in 1923, English Electric Wren number 4, was the joint overall winner of the economy contest. The Vickers Viget sits in the background. VIA PHILIP JARRETT

perches herself on the back or the owner buys a two-seater. And as one cannot perch a passenger on the back of a motorglider it follows that the light aeroplane of the future must be a two-seater."

In any case, Grey doubted "very much whether there can be much of a market for privately-owned light aeroplanes. The makers may produce two-seaters for the benefit of the designing female aforesaid, but even then it is hardly likely that enough can be sold to make them worth while. The trouble is that they have to be flown from an aerodrome of some sort and they cannot be run out of a garage like a car and started straight away on a journey.

"Some few landed gentry may have usable aerodromes in their own parks just outside their hall-doors and their sons may take a fancy to flying motorgliders. But the number of such sportsmen cannot be large. Here and there small flying clubs may be formed near big towns where the sons of well-to-do merchants may run several machines on the co-operative principle. But even in this way the demand cannot be considerable as a factory proposition...

"Also, nothing is so boring as flying after use has worn away the first novel sensations. When that stage is passed flying becomes simply a quick and comfortable way of getting about the country. And the man who can only afford a motorglider cannot afford to spend half of his time touring about the country for fun. Therefore the motorglider must spend most of its time doing nothing. Which is a bad investment."

But if Grey's underlying rationale was deeply anachronistic, the ability for a light aeroplane to carry more than just its pilot would indeed prove desirable. And few could argue with his remark that, "despite the high performances which were got out of the machines at Lympne it was evident that none of them could be made into two-seaters and remain a useful vehicle. Nor, indeed, that "the motor-cycle engine is neither big enough nor reliable enough for a flying machine when judged by the standards of the modern aero-engine."

It had been the Duke of Sutherland, then Under-Secretary of State for Air in Stanley Baldwin's first government and vice-president of the Royal Aero Club, who kick-started the Lympne contests. Following on from the club's gliding competition at Itford Hill in the summer of 1922, he was the driving force behind a £500 official award for the most economical British aircraft in an equivalent event aimed at what were termed "low-powered aeroplanes". That definition was kept deliberately loose, but given the 750cc maximum engine capacity, power outputs would remain strictly limited. Specifically, the winner would be the machine that completed the most laps of a 12.5-mile course on one gallon of petrol. The *Daily Mail* pledged £1,000 to the victor, this time no matter which country it hailed from. Sundry other monetary prizes were offered for the best speed, distance, height, short landing and overall lap count.

Before flying, each entrant had to undergo several ground transportation tests. These, said Grey, "consisted of taking the wings off the machines and transporting them and the rest of the machine through a gate into a field and back, a distance of a mile, in three hours". And while being moved by road, each aircraft was not to occupy "more than half of a fifteen-foot roadway."

From the moment they began, at 07.00hrs on Monday 8 October, ➤

representatives of *The Aeroplane* were among those gathered at Lympne to witness proceedings. The journal's contest diary provides a splendid period account of a pioneering occasion.

Monday 8 October

On English Electric Wren number 4, Flt Lt Walter Longton was first into the air for an economy run. In a light wind, he proceeded to complete several circuits of the course, covering 87.5 miles and spending two hours 40 minutes aloft. *The Aeroplane* reported, "on the last leg of the last lap he finished his gallon and turned on his spare pint. He landed and went into the measuring hangar to have his consumption measured and worked out by Dr A. R. Low who was the official measurer. Shortly after it was

> ❝ *Interest centred on the 'Snakes and Ladders' Competition* ❞

announced that he had done 80.3 miles per gallon."

Could others do better? With the second Wren, Sqn Ldr Maurice Wright notched up 71mpg, Fred Raynham on the Handasyde 65.7, Bert Hinkler on the Avro 560 monoplane 54.6, Geoffrey de Havilland on the DH53 50.8 and Maj Harold Hemming on a similar machine 50. Capt Norman Macmillan suffered engine trouble on the Parnall Pixie and achieved 49mpg. Early attempts on the speed prize saw an ANEC I reaching 66.5mph with Jimmy James up, and Hemming 57.5mph on the DH53. Harold Hamersley's Avro 558 biplane laid down a marker for the height contest at 6,300ft, as well as "flying up and down for some considerable time with both his hands above his head."

The Vickers Viget, flown by Stan Cockerell, had a troubled outing: "after a couple of circuits he had a forced landing near Brabourne. He folded the wings of the machine himself and then proceeded to push it home six miles along the road. It is said that in one place he stopped at a 'rest house' for refreshment in his arduous labour and when he came out he found a number of people waiting who asked him when the performance was going to start. On asking what they meant he was informed that they were under the impression that the object that he was pushing was a Punch and Judy Show."

Tuesday 9 October

James, flying early and "in quite a strong wind", set a new 87.5mpg benchmark with an ANEC. This went unbeaten for the remainder of the event, only being equalled. Otherwise, "Nothing very exciting happened on Tuesday and interest was chiefly centred in what was dubbed the 'Snakes and Ladders' Competition", for "the machine that covered the greatest number of laps. If a machine piled up say 30 laps and then a portion of the machine or engine had to be changed the pilot had to go back again to the beginning and start again". Hinkler with the Avro monoplane, Hemming on the DH53, and James and Maurice Piercey flying the ANEC were the main protagonists. "The competition waxed fast and furious and all three machines kept within a lap of one another until at lunch time Major Hemming broke a crankshaft, 'got on the head of a snake' and so had to go back to the beginning."

Wednesday 10 October

Despite "squalls and gusty rains", Longton flew Wren number 4 in the morning and achieved a fuel consumption figure of 90.5mpg. However, "as he had to land after five circuits and did not use the whole of his gallon this figure could not stand". Conditions were far from easy, and Rex Stocken force-landed his Gnosspelius Gull. It remained undamaged and was returned to Lympne by road.

While all this was going on, Hinkler "was steadily going round and round the course piling up laps in the 'Snakes and Ladders' Competition in which he was now leading easily. About midday the wind dropped and a thick fog with a visibility of 100 yards came down. This did not seem to worry Mr Hinkler in the very least and he went on steadily until Mr A. V. Roe grew anxious as to his safety. Finally Mr Roe could stand it no longer and when next Mr Hinkler appeared Mr Roe with one accord dashed out onto the aerodrome and shouted him down."

Larry Carter got airborne in the Gloucestershire Gannet, on which the two-stroke Carden engine had been playing up. "Mr Carter took off in the direction of the sea and as he got over the cliff the mist closed right down. Much anxiety was felt for his safety but after about ten minutes he appeared from the other direction and landed safely. Had the engine been running properly this little machine would no doubt have given a brilliant account of itself. Both for workmanship and general lines it was one of the prettiest machines present."

Steadily the weather worsened, and a degree of chaos set in. "At about two o'clock the wind sprang up and cleared the fog but the wind went on rising until by 14.30 hours it had touched gale force. Just before the fog Major Hemming flew past the enclosure and shouted down that Mr Broad had had a forced landing and it was ascertained that the reason for this was a broken rocker-arm. He also located one or two other machines which were lost on the ground in the fog. When the gale was at its height Major Hemming with the spare rocker flew off and dropped this to Mr Broad who after 20 minutes or so effected his repair and flew back to the aerodrome. The way the two de Havillands flew and landed in the gale was perfectly ❯

The Avro 560 was the sole example of this attractive monoplane ever built. It was evaluated by the Air Ministry after the contest, but not procured. VIA PHILIP JARRETT

Bert Hinkler was almost constantly airborne in the Avro 560 when conditions allowed. VIA PHILIP JARRETT

Folding wings were a feature of the Gloucestershire Gannet, but good performance was not. VIA PHILIP JARRETT

LYMPNE 1923: RUNNERS AND RIDERS

Entry number	Aircraft	Engine	Pilot(s)	Results
2	Gnosspelius Gull G-EBGN	698cc Blackburne Tomtit	John Lankester Parker	Speed: 55.25mph
3	English Electric Wren G-EBNV	400cc ABC	Sqn Ldr Maurice Wright	Consumption: 82.5mpg Mileage: 175 miles (14 laps)
4	English Electric Wren	400cc ABC	Flt Lt Walter Longton	Consumption: 87.5mpg — tied with number 18 for Sutherland and *Daily Mail* prizes, £750 Mileage: 362 miles (29 laps)
5	A. V. Roe and Co Model 558	B and H	Bert Hinkler	No official figures; flew very little
6	A. V. Roe and Co Model 560	698cc Blackburne Tomtit	Bert Hinkler	Consumption: 63.3mpg Mileage: 1,000 miles (80 laps) — winner of trophies for most laps and longest distance, £300
7	Gloucestershire Gannet G-EBHU	Carden	Larry Carter	Flew but engine trouble prevented official tests
8	de Havilland DH53 G-EBHX	750cc Douglas	Capt Geoffrey de Havilland and Capt Hubert Broad	Consumption: 50.8mpg Mileage: 100 miles (eight laps)
9	Parnall Pixie G-EBKM	500cc Douglas	Capt Norman Macmillan	Consumption: 53.4mpg Mileage: 125 miles (10 laps)
10	Vickers Viget G-EBHN	750cc Douglas	Capt Stan Cockerell	Speed: 58.1mph
11	A. V. Roe and Co Model 558 G-EBHW	500cc Douglas	Capt Harold Hamersley	Altitude: 13,850ft — second altitude prize, £100
12	de Havilland DH53 G-EBHZ	750cc Douglas	Maj Harold Hemming	Consumption: 59.3mpg Mileage: 387 miles (31 laps)
13	Handasyde monoplane	750cc Douglas	Fred Raynham	Consumption: 65.7mpg Mileage: 162 miles (13 laps)
14	RAE Aero Club Hurricane G-EBHS	600cc Douglas	Flt Lt 'George' Bulman	Speed: 58.5mph
15	Peyret monoplane	748cc Sergant	Alexis Maneyrol	Altitude: 9,400ft
16	Poncelet Vivette O-BAFH	748cc Sergant	Baron Georges Kervyn de Lettenhove	No figures
17	ANEC I G-EBIL	698cc Blackburne Tomtit	Jimmy James and Maurice Piercey	Cracked a cylinder early in the meeting and thereafter kept in reserve to No 18
18	ANEC I G-EBHR	698cc Blackburne Tomtit	Jimmy James and Maurice Piercey	Consumption: 87.5mpg — tied with number 4 for Sutherland and *Daily Mail* prizes, £750 Mileage: 775 miles (62 laps) Speed: 74mph Altitude: 14,400ft — winner of altitude prize
19	Gnosspelius Gull	698cc Blackburne Tomtit	Capt Rex Stocken	No figures
21	Poncelet Castar O-BAFG	748cc Sergant	Victor Simonet	Speed: 58.1mph
24	Parnall Pixie MkII G-EBKN	750cc Douglas	Capt Norman Macmillan	Speed: 76.5mph — winner of speed prize, £500
25	Sayers-Handley Page monoplane	400cc ABC	Gordon Olley	Mileage: 37.5 (three laps)

Note: the missing numbers in the above sequence, and those from 26-28, relate to aircraft that were entered but did not show up

extraordinary and both pilots were congratulated on their flights by the Duke of Sutherland."

Thursday 11 October

Again starting early, Longton once more showed the performance of the Wren, equalling James's 87.5mpg. The weather thereafter precluded any serious attempts on their fuel consumption benchmark, though the Sayers-Handley Page HP22 — erected overnight and put through its transport tests that morning — looked as if it might challenge. "It had been arranged", said the report, "that the machine should be catapulted off the ground in the manner of the gliders at Itford Hill last year... She was lapping in about 16 minutes and it appeared as though she would be a very dangerous competitor in the consumption test but half-way round the third circuit a rocker-bracket worked loose and in that condition Mr Olley who was flying her brought her back to within a few yards of the aerodrome just failing to get over the final fence, a performance which showed that she had a very high efficiency."

The Parnall Pixie had been transformed overnight from number 9 to number 24, "by taking off the big wings and fitting a smaller pair — and taking out the low-powered Douglas and fitting a bigger one. The performance of the machine was watched with much interest as few people believed that it could possibly fly with so little surface. However it took off in a surprisingly short distance and proved to be very manoeuvrable in the air. Mr Macmillan completed the two circuits necessary for the speed flight at 76 miles an hour though on the straight the machine must have been doing very nearly a hundred and finished with a beautiful landing". Later it was reconverted to its previous configuration for the fuel consumption attempt, but the weather prevented this, so it was changed back again.

Friday 12 October

"Owing to the gale and the storm", *The Aeroplane* recorded, "there was no flying on Friday and interest was centred on the sea."

Saturday 13 October

The climactic day, and a tragic one, with the death of Alexis Maneyrol in the Peyret monoplane. In the morning he had snatched the lead of the altitude contest, at 9,500ft. After Piercey and Hamersley went still higher, Maneyrol tried again. As he came in to land, "at a hundred feet or so both wings folded back simultaneously and the machine fell like a rocket-stick. Officials and doctors rushed across to the spot but M. Maneyrol died a few minutes later. There is very little doubt that the machine was of too weak a construction and one was informed by an official of the Air Ministry that if competing machines had had to be passed as airworthy before they were allowed to fly the Peyret machine would not have been allowed to ascend."

It had earlier appeared as if Baron Georges Kervyn de Lettenhove might become the meeting's first casualty, when his Poncelot Vivette monoplane "was beaten down to the ground. A wing-tip caught the ground and the machine turned clean over. It looked like a serious accident at first, but the bold Baron crawled out completely unhurt and like Oliver Twist asked for more. Unfortunately, a completely casséed rudder foiled his ambitions."

❖

As the day wore on, and time ran out for any further tilts at the economy prizes, more attention turned to the speed and altitude contests. While Macmillan reached 82mph on a test circuit, the Pixie's Douglas engine "gave trouble" half-way round his second official lap, leading to a forced landing. He still ran out the winner on speed, however, the 78mph he set on Thursday going unbeaten.

Unwanted excitement was caused mid-afternoon, when Raynham's Handasyde, Hemming's DH53 and the ANEC of Piercey "were all seen to be coming down together with their airscrews stationary". *The Aeroplane*'s correspondent suggested to an official that those aircraft sitting in front of the public enclosure should be moved to prevent their being damaged in the event of landing mishaps, or people sent out to form a protective cordon. "Piercey coming down numbed with cold overshot his landing and went straight at the waiting machines. Mr A. B. Rogers the representative of British Petroleum petrol at Croydon who was looking after the firm's interests at Lympne pluckily stood in the way of a wing tip of the machine and swung it round so that the nose of Mr

The Parnall Pixie in its large-winged configuration, with contest number 9. VIA PHILIP JARRETT

Of three Sayers-Handley Page monoplanes entered, only number 25 took part, Gordon Olley at the controls. VIA PHILIP JARRETT

Piercey's machine only caught the tailplane of Mr Broad's de Havilland and damaged it slightly, very slightly damaging a wing of Mr Piercey's machine also… Mr Rogers got a bad bump in the chest which laid him out for the moment but he soon recovered."

Before all that, Piercey had been to 14,500ft and Hamersley to 14,000. Maneyrol's accident led to the abandonment of the planned formal dinner and ceremony that evening, but there was an informal prizegiving at Lord Edward Grosvenor's home. Having just missed out on the altitude award, Hamersley received a second prize of £100 for his efforts, rustled up by the Duke of Sutherland and other Royal Aero Club members.

Inevitably, some of the aircraft impressed more than others. Not among the official winners, the DH53s gained many plaudits, not least for Hubert Broad's displays, described as including "looping, rolling and, spinning as though ❯

it were any ordinary high-powered aeroplane". *The Aeroplane* added, "It seems a pity that the two de Havillands were not awarded a special prize for general utility as their general handiness, controllability, and flying qualities singled them out for very special comment. Nevertheless it seems probable that they will reap their reward in orders". The reporter cited talk of potential RAF training use. C. G. Grey's summation was pithy: they were, he opined, "the best all-round machines of the Meeting", but "not powerful enough for the Speed Prize", "not 'cleaned-up' enough for the Consumption Prize", and "not light enough for the Altitude Prize."

The Wrens, too, caught the collective attention. Langton's "wonderful exhibition of his famous crazy flying [...] utterly startled everybody who had no idea that [it] had such wonderful qualities as a flying machine. The lack of noise from the little ABC engine and the curious antics of the machine irresistibly reminded one of a moth fluttering round a candle". As Grey pointed out, "They are not and do not pretend to be all-weather cross-country machines". But, he felt, "a

> ## 66 *No one of them was a freak in general design* 99

modified motorglider of a similar type with a bigger engine would be a very nice flying machine..."

In their debut showings, the ANEC Is illustrated the ability of the Air Navigation and Engineering Company's William Shackleton.

"They were designed and built for aerodynamic efficiency and they achieve the designer's object", remarked Grey. "The pilot is tucked away right inside the fuselage and has in consequence a very limited outlook ahead and none at all upwards so they are not ideal cross-country machines. But they do fly amazingly well". He marvelled at how the ANECs, with a 698cc engine, both matched the 87.5mpg of the smaller-engined Wren and got to 15,000ft. Similarly, the Pixie was the first civilian aircraft conceived by Parnall company designer Harold Bolas, and "well deserved the speed prize."

Avro's offerings managed fine feats of flying, the 560 monoplane's success in the aggregate mileage stakes being down, Grey wrote, to the "energy and determination" of Hinkler in continuing trouble-free lappery through all weathers. Yet it was, he commented, "a very good practical cross-country machine". The Douglas-engined 558 biplane "was taken to amazing heights" by Hamersley, whose airmanship also attracted significant admiration.

What of the rest? Grey concluded of the Handasyde, "There is nothing startling about it, but it does fly thoroughly well". He thought much the same of Vickers' Viget: it "flew excellently but not quite well enough to win anything". The small team from the RAE Aero Club created in the Hurricane "a machine for a trained pilot", but one in need of a bigger engine. Given the greater experience of Oscar Gnosspelius, the Gull "hardly came up to expectations". It "seemed to be unduly tricky to control, especially fore and aft". Maladies afflicting the Gloucestershire Gannet's Carden motor kept it largely ground-bound. The Sayers-Handley Page monoplane, later dubbed the HP22, "had been altered a good deal from the original design and it evidently needs to be re-altered before it will fly well". Belgium's Poncelet monoplanes were "a distinct credit to their country… their general design and construction are good". On the subject of the ill-fated Peyret, Grey felt it "as well to say as little as possible."

The previous year's Itford glider meeting — apart from being announced at short notice and attracting few entries — had been notable for the outlandish, or downright poor-quality, designs on display. Lympne, with certain exceptions, saw little of that. Even Grey acknowledged, "Taking them all round the machines were a very good lot". *The Aeroplane*'s technical editor William H. Sayers noted, "Very few machines showed any abnormality in the design or proportion of their control surfaces, and no British machines showed any sign of lack of control. The majority showed abnormal controllability."

❖

Sayers might not be considered an entirely independent observer. A pioneering aircraft designer, he had penned the three Sayers-Handley Page machines entered, only one of which was present at Lympne. But he was right, and he gave credit to all those British firms who took part, contributing 16 aeroplanes of 12 distinct types. "No one of them was a freak in general design, yet no one of them was uninteresting, and among them those 16 machines have made the efforts of other nations to produce light aeroplanes look distinctly feeble. Purely and simply from a sporting point of view this result is thoroughly and entirely gratifying. But there is more to it than the sporting side for the light aeroplane presents all the technical problems of the normal aeroplane together with some of its own."

Flight was more optimistic than *The Aeroplane* about the prospects for such aircraft. "While fully realising the as yet untouched possibilities of the use by the RAF of the light 'plane, we do not think for a moment that its usefulness ends there", a post-Lympne comment piece said. "To the private owner-pilot of moderate means the type offers unlimited possibilities. Not expensive in first cost, and very cheap to operate, the light 'plane should appeal to hundreds of sportsmen at home, while in the Colonies and Dominions, where roads are none too good and railways few and far between, the light 'plane should prove a boon to land owners residing far from the nearest town". A further-sighted assessment than Grey's, certainly — and one much closer to the mark.

There was still much work to do. Straight after 1923's contest, the Duke of Sutherland confirmed a £500 prize for the winner of the 1924 edition, which would be contested by two-seat light aeroplanes. The Air Ministry promised money, too. The truly practical light aircraft for recreational and training purposes remained a little way off, and the constraints of the Lympne trials' rules arguably too rigid to further the cause of such a design. But 1923 had been a start down the right road, even if not everybody appreciated it. **A**

Another Avro Success!

Light Aeroplane Competitions at Lympne, October 8-13, 1923.

The Avro Monoplane Motor Glider.

IN the Light Aeroplane Competitions, held at Lympne October 8th and 13th, the Avro Monoplane Motor Glider, Type 560, fitted with a 6 h.p. Blackburne engine, piloted by B. Hinkler, won the prizes presented by the S.M.M. & T. and B.C. & M.C. & M.C.M. & T.U. Ltd., for the greatest number of completed circuits of the course, by flying 80 circuits, representing 1,000 miles.

THIS feat was carried out under the most adverse weather conditions, and gives infallible proof of the airworthiness of this wonderful little machine.

IN the ALTITUDE COMPETITION the Avro Biplane Motor Glider, Type 558, fitted with a 500 c.c. Douglas engine, piloted by F/O Hamersley, was awarded second prize. It attained an altitude of 13,850 feet which constitutes a record for a machine fitted with a 500 c.c. engine.

THESE successes prove once more the reliability of Avro machines, and uphold the manufacturers' reputation as the pioneers in the design and construction of the world's best aircraft.

A. V. ROE & Co., Ltd.
Avro Works, Newton Heath.
MANCHESTER.

London Offices:
166, PICCADILLY, W.1.

Experimental Works:
HAMBLE, SOUTHAMPTON.

The Avro Biplane Motor Glider.

The D.H. Type 53

736 c.c. DOUGLAS ENGINE *or* 698 BLACKBURN ENGINE

"THE two De Havilland 53s, were by general opinion considered to be the best all-round machines of the meeting, which was why they won no prizes. They were not powerful enough for the Speed Prize. They were not "cleaned up" enough for the Consumption Prize. They were not light enough for the Altitude Prize. But in spite of that there is no doubt that for design, construction, finish, detail work, controllability and general flyableness, there was nothing at Lympne which quite reached so high an average on all points. So here was another score for one of the great pioneers of aviation, seeing that Capt. de Havilland has been flying continuously since 1909."

C. G. GREY, *Editor*, THE AEROPLANE, *Oct. 17th, 1923.*

"THERE is no doubt whatever that of all the machines at Lympne the D.H.53 was the nearest approach to a really practicable type of single-seater for all-round use. Its handiness both on the ground and in the air was astonishing for so small a machine. Actually these machines should not be regarded as competition machines at all, but rather as samples of what the owner-pilot may safely expect of a light aeroplane and also of what can be produced in the way of a light, cheap and simple training machine which is nevertheless capable of being used for quite advanced flying in even very bad weather.
There seems no reason whatever why D.H.53s fitted with camera guns should not be used for the first training of single-seat fighter pilots in gunnery and fighting tactics, for they possess the quality of rapidity of manoeuvre to a degree not excelled by any actual fighter one has yet seen. In construction the D.H.53 is notable for its complete lack of freakishness. It is a simple but extremely sound example of standard British methods of construction carried out on a reduced scale."

Capt. W. H. SAYERS, *Technical Editor*, THE AEROPLANE, *Oct. 24th, 1923.*

"THE De Havilland 53 light aeroplane with 6 h.p. motor-cycle engine . . . . no other country has a machine that can approach the De Havilland for general utility, strength, workmanship and manoeuvrability."

THE AEROPLANE, *Oct. 31st, 1923.*

THE DE HAVILLAND AIRCRAFT CO. LTD.
STAG LANE AERODROME.
EDGWARE, MIDDLESEX.

Telegrams—"Havilland, Edgware."
Telephone—Kingsbury 160-164.

DH

BELOW LEFT: Among the stranger designs was the Gnosspelius Gull, of which two were on the entry list. Number 19 was handled by Rex Stocken, but only briefly. KEY COLLECTION

BELOW: Alexis Maneyrol, a noted gliding pioneer, in the cockpit of the Peyret monoplane just before his fatal flight. TOPFOTO

THE 'OLDST

The recently declassified reports from Project 'Oldster', the RAF element of the CIA's U-2 programme, reveal more detail on life with the Turkey-based detachment than has ever been public before

WORDS: BEN DUNNELL

"At the moment I am only writing to let you know that we arrived securely and are busy settling in. There were no big snags on the way out. We were delayed five hours for fog and arrived in Ankara in the early hours. It's as well we were met as, of course, the hotel had never heard of us and we had to go elsewhere!"

It sounds like a holiday postcard, but it's marked 'Top Secret' and is, in fact, the first — informal — report back to the Air Ministry from one of the RAF's most clandestine operational commitments. The author is given as Mr M. G. Bradley, writing from Adana, Turkey on 20 November 1958. To be more accurate, he was Flt Lt Michael Bradley, one of four RAF pilots then assigned to fly the Lockheed U-2 with the US Central Intelligence Agency, under the cover of working as civilians for the Meteorological Office. His handwritten note was addressed to the Air Ministry, and specifically Wg Cdr Colin Kunkler, the staff officer in the Directorate of Operations — Bomber and Reconnaissance. This, too, was a euphemistic title. Kunkler was the deputy head of the cell charged with overseeing Project 'Oldster', the British government codename for RAF involvement with the U-2.

The fact of 'Oldster's' existence has been known for a long while. So have many details relating to it. Yet most of those came not from declassified UK archives, but other sources. U-2 expert Chris Pocock's books and official CIA histories were foremost among them. When during 1998 the agency published its first detailed account of its role with the U-2, it was heavily redacted. Subsequent efforts using the US Freedom of Information Act resulted, 15 years later, in that document being published in far more complete form. Then in 2016 there emerged a 2,500-page in-house history of the CIA's Office of Special Activities, under whose remit U-2 operations fell. In each case significant new information came forth, but still the UK was reluctant to be similarly amenable, bar the opening of the odd non-specific file. The two-part article in the January and February 2019 issues of this magazine was written on that basis.

But there was clearly much more to come. After we went to press

The only known image of a CIA U-2 during a deployment to Britain to establish the weather research cover story for the type's operations: U-2A 56-6682, or Article 349, at Watton in — probably — May 1959 with the fictitious tail number '417'. NATIONAL ARCHIVES

ER' DIARIES

with those features, this author's freedom of information request to the UK Ministry of Defence bore fruit. A huge collection of documents — 23 in all, numbering some 2,700 pages — was released to the National Archives. They revealed many hitherto unknown details, whether on policy or operations. And in the detachment reports, mostly despatched from Turkey to London on a monthly basis, are contained more discursive accounts of 'Oldster' life, in the air and on the ground.

This diary, not previously published to any great degree, begins by covering the period from 21 November-4 December 1958. However, the background dates to January 1956 and a visit to London by Richard M. Bissell Jr, boss of the CIA's Project 'Aquatone', as the agency dubbed its U-2 programme. Lockheed's ground-breaking high-altitude reconnaissance platform was still undergoing flight-testing, and Bissell sounded the UK out about providing a future operating base, not least for overflights of the Soviet Union. He met the head of

MI6, Sir John Sinclair, and the RAF's deputy chief of the air staff, both offering their support. So did the Foreign Secretary, Selwyn Lloyd. Indications that the Americans would be happy to share intelligence from U-2 sorties no doubt helped oil the wheels. RAF Lakenheath would house the CIA's Detachment A, four

U-2s duly being transported to the Suffolk base to begin training flights under the guise of performing high-altitude weather research.

The subsequent story was covered in more depth in our January 2019 issue — how a change of heart by Prime Minister Anthony Eden led to the rapid abandonment of British >

From left to right, Sqn Ldr Christopher Walker and Flt Lts John MacArthur, Michael Bradley and David Dowling were the first four RAF U-2 pilots, pictured during training in 1958. VIA CHRIS POCOCK

ABOVE: Training of the initial British contingent — and the three groups of RAF pilots that followed — was undertaken by the US Air Force's 4080th Strategic Reconnaissance Wing at Laughlin AFB, Texas, on U-2As such as **56-6696.** USAF

basing and the CIA detachment's first operational missions being mounted from Wiesbaden, West Germany; how discussions began about using British pilots; and how it was agreed to train an initial cadre of four Britons on the type. Sqn Ldr Christopher Walker and Flt Lts Michael Bradley, David Dowling and John MacArthur duly underwent check-out in June-July 1958. This was a US Air Force responsibility, being performed by Strategic Air Command's 4080th Strategic Reconnaissance Wing at Laughlin AFB near Del Rio, Texas. Walker lost his life in the crash of a U-2A on 8 July, after it went out of control at altitude on a training sortie. In due course, he was replaced as RAF detachment commander by Sqn Ldr Robbie Robinson.

Thus was composed the British contingent that deployed to Adana — better-known now as Incirlik — as part of the CIA's existing Detachment B. With the approval of Eden's successor as Prime Minister, Harold Macmillan, and US President Dwight D. Eisenhower, the way was clear for RAF pilots to fly the U-2 operationally. And this is where the diary begins.

> **❝ *Whether the det helped our cover story is open to conjecture* ❞**

21 November-5 December 1958

"Colonel Beerli returned on 28 November and our U-2 flying began immediately", wrote Bradley. "We were all a trifle apprehensive of our first ride, wondering how rusty we had become on leave. Pilots here are left much more to rely on their own judgement on landing than they were at Del Rio, owing for the need for radio security. There is no one calling out your heights or hold-off as we had become used to. However, we all made it without bending any valuable machinery… Since then Dowling and Bradley have carried out two 4-hour training missions each. These have been around the 'local area', covering most of Turkey and as far west as Athens. [Assessment] of accuracy has been hampered by cloud cover but results so far have been quite good."

Incidentally, Col Stan Beerli was the Detachment B commander, on secondment to the CIA from the USAF. In general, Bradley said, "the informal atmosphere and lack of restrictive regulations compared to our experience in SAC was refreshing". He and his British colleagues appreciated the chance to conduct continuation flying on the detachment's three Lockheed T-33s, and, he added, "All of us are finding the civilian way of life and approach to the job a bit strange and rather pleasant."

January 1959

Not recorded here, for some reason, is the December 1958 deployment to Britain. It saw two U-2s being detached from Adana to RAF Watton, Norfolk for meteorological research missions, this largely as a means of establishing the Met Office cover story. Only one was carried out, due to poor weather. But the operational tasking had now been clarified. Agreement was reached for sorties to be flown by the RAF pilots from UK bases as well as those overseas, while Macmillan wrote to Eisenhower on 10 December to approve an initial programme of Middle East reconnaissances by the 'Oldster' pilots, each individual flight being subject to the PM's approval.

So, wrote Robinson — who had arrived on 2 January — "All pilots have accomplished at least one M.E. [Middle East] flight, with varying degrees of success. Weather and auto-pilot malfunction have plagued most of the flights". MacArthur was the first RAF pilot to fly a CIA U-2 mission, photographing objectives in Egypt, Syria and Jordan on 31 December 1958. Then came Bradley on 10 January 1959, capturing images over Egypt, Jordan and Iraq, followed by Robinson on the 13th, his sortie taking in Syria, Egypt and Saudi Arabia. "It has been interesting to observe and experience the reaction of flying over the Middle Eastern area", Robinson remarked, "for this in a small way is going to be similar to genuine overflight [of the Soviet Union]. Although the territory one is flying over is denied, it is known that opposition is either non existent or inferior..."

In that context, CIA archives detail British concerns about the U-2's possible vulnerability to evolving Soviet air defences. The latest intelligence and information on zoom climb tests, those documents say, "cleared the air and improved the outlook of the 'Oldster' pilots toward flying the U-2", but it is interesting that discussion of this subject merits no mention in the dispatches from Adana.

February 1959

Five operational taskings over the Middle East, known as headquarters-directed missions, were scheduled. All were cancelled, Robinson reported, "for either lack of political approval, or unfavourable weather and contrail [forecasts] along the route". In addition, plans for Soviet overflights set to start mid-month were put on the back-burner when Macmillan visited Moscow for talks with Soviet premier Nikita Khrushchev. Training details were flown instead, while T-33 continuation flying was a welcome chance "to 'let off steam', and to do two things which have

become quite a novelty — to fly close to the ground and to pull 'g' without endangering the back end of the aircraft!"

May 1959

While March had seen one short Middle East mission, and April two, May brought a highlight in the form of Operation 'Gay Blade', another deployment to Watton. This was much more successful than December's, generating two weather reconnaissance flights by a single aircraft. "Whether the detachment helped our cover story is open to conjecture", mused Robinson. "A large proportion of the weather package was inoperative and our length of stay hardly gave time for our presence to be felt". However, it did allow the CIA to exercise the 'Fast Move' concept for rapid U-2 deployments. Only an emergency landing at Brize Norton by the aircraft involved, which suffered a hydraulic failure while being flown by MacArthur, put a spanner in the works. It was rapidly repaired. Back at Adana, Robinson notched up "a well flown Middle East flight."

June 1959

A trio of Middle East missions experienced mixed fortunes. Flying across the Sinai on 4 June, Bradley "passed four miles inside the Israeli border", 24 miles from his intended track. All pilots were re-briefed on the need to avoid Israel's airspace. Dowling aborted his 26 June tasking due to contrails, but it was reflown by MacArthur, only for the film from the B-configuration Hycon high-altitude camera, of 36in focal length, to be destroyed during processing.

July 1959

As American pilot Marty Knutson conducted a USSR overflight on 9 July, operating out of Peshawar, Pakistan to capture Hycon B camera imagery of the Soviet missile test facility at Tyuratam — also known as the Baikonur Cosmodrome — and covering other important targets in going all the way to Sverdlovsk, so the British contingent sat forlornly at Adana. Robinson recounted, "we were not informed about it prior to it taking place, although the activity surrounding pre-operation build up was difficult to conceal from other members of the detachment and speculation was rife. Naturally the Oldster personnel were keenly disappointed that they were not participating in the operation and a temporary drop in morale was [apparent]. We had always felt that in spite of the politicians this mission would be flown by us and a certain loss of face was inevitable". They could only reflect on how, hopefully, their time was to come — and on a Middle East sortie by Robinson, with "lengthy coverage" of Syria, Iraq and Saudi Arabia.

August 1959

A pair of Middle East flights aside, the focus was on aircraft re-equipment as Detachment B's U-2As gave way to two new U-2Cs, fitted with the Pratt & Whitney J75-P-13 engine instead of the earlier J57-P-37. Pilot views were mixed. Robinson described its performance as "most impressive", noting the "very apparent" 4,800lb thrust increase and a service ceiling increased by some 4-5,000ft. Against that, he pointed out "a reduction in range performance when cruise- ➲

BELOW:
In U-2A form, serial 56-6681 served with CIA Detachment A at Lakenheath, Wiesbaden and Giebelstadt during 1956-57. By the time this image was taken, it had been converted into a U-2C and registered N801X. CIA

climbing at maximum permissible power", due to "the increase in drag at the very high lift coefficient at which the aircraft is operating… at reduced power height can be sacrificed to increase the range, if circumstances permit."

Above all, Robinson said, "the aircraft is only as good as the end result", and a full operating capability had yet to be achieved. "Difficulty was encountered in fitting the various systems into the equipment-bay and local modifications were necessary before this could be done. A rather astounding omission was the lack of an alternator for the provision of AC current for the ELINT [electronic intelligence-gathering] systems. The alternator was fitted to the engine here at 'B' but is not working satisfactorily". For the pilots, "the increased thrust and performance […] resulted in the flight profile being very close to the [aircraft's] limiting envelope". This rendered an accurate autopilot "essential", for hand-flying the U-2C at altitude required "undivided attention."

September-October 1959

Although a single Middle East sortie was flown prior to 23 September, on that date Parliament was dissolved prior to the upcoming general election, and 'Oldster' headquarters-directed flights were suspended for the duration of the campaign. Macmillan was returned to power by the 8 October poll, allowing a resumption of mission approvals six days later. However, the election did not prevent a third 'cover story' deployment to Watton, Operation 'Fullhouse', from 3-7 October. Two weather flights were completed, and the 'Fast Move' arrangements exercised.

Activity was soon to step up significantly. On 28 October, Robinson wrote, "approval was received for Oldster participation in ELINT flights. The immediate significance of the approval is that we can now fly the System 7 missions gathering data from the Russian ICBM [intercontinental ballistic missile] and associated space programmes". System VII, as it was more officially dubbed, was a sensor developed by HRB-Singer and used from high altitude to acquire telemetry from the likes of ICBM and satellite launches. First employed on 9 June, it could record information on up to six frequencies for a period of 12 minutes.

"Since the introduction of this system", continued Robinson, "a considerable proportion of the detachment effort has been devoted to it, and a continuous standby of personnel involved is maintained, due to the usually limited alert period possible on these missions. It is felt that our participation will assist materially in the overall effort, as well as giving our pilots more experience and a greater feeling of usefulness". It required them to become night-qualified on the U-2, rather than just the T-33 as was the case at this point, but no great stumbling-block was foreseen.

Robinson expected readiness for the ELINT task by the second week of November.

On 30 October, meanwhile, "two Oldster missions were flown simultaneously over the Iraq and Egyptian areas. This was to obtain a total aircraft count". While "first reports from URPIC [the processing and interpretation centre] indicated good results on each flight", part of the coverage from Dowling's sortie was lost due to a lack of film.

November 1959

"Notification was received from Headquarters of the possibility of an Oldster overflight in the near future using the U-2s", noted Robinson, so all the RAF pilots carried out fuel consumption checks on both U-2Cs employing the 71,000ft mission profile. "The results all agreed to within 10 gallons with flights over eight hours, and compared favourably with the handbook figures. There was little to choose between the two aircraft, 351 and 358. If anything 358 produced the better fuel curves and it was decided to use this aircraft for the mission."

But while no overflight took place for now, on 20 November there occurred the first System VII ELINT mission by an 'Oldster' pilot, Dowling doing the honours. "Although no visual sighting of the missile was made there were indications of a lock-on which were later verified. The mission was considered highly successful, and the important time check given by the pilot […] brought forth compliments from Headquarters."

December 1959

It was the moment all the 'Oldster' pilots had been waiting for: the first overflight of the Soviet Union by a U-2 in the hands of an RAF pilot. The date was 6 December, and Robinson was at the controls for what was codenamed Operation 'High Wire', otherwise referred to as Mission B 8005. It followed a hiatus in overflights that had lasted since 9 July, deliberately taking in the period before and after Khrushchev's historic US visit during September. Now, with approval from Macmillan, Britain was ready to step into the breach. It represented quite a political risk for the PM, not least since he had agreed with Eisenhower that responsibility in the event of an incident would be taken on by whichever country's pilot was flying.

According to Robinson, notification of the mission was received at 19.30hrs Zulu time on 4 December. Three-quarters of an hour later, both he and secondary pilot MacArthur saw the route and studied the primary targets. Demonstrating just what was meant by 'Fast Move', at 22.20 Zulu a C-130 Hercules left Adana with the three-man 'Oldster' contingent — Robinson, MacArthur and navigator/mission planner Flt Lt Collingwood — on board, together with accompanying equipment. "Both pilots had space to sleep on the trip", wrote Robinson, for despite the C-130's lack of passenger comfort they used "a combination of sedatives and warm sleeping bags."

Via a short refuelling stop in Bahrain, the transport landed in Peshawar at 10.00 Zulu on the 5th. The U-2, meanwhile, was flown in from Turkey during the hours of darkness. Using the Pakistani base rather than Adana for USSR overflights took advantage of a gap in Soviet early-warning radar coverage. The cargo was offloaded into a Pakistan Air Force hangar, affording ample time for the two pilots to study both route and target maps.

Again they enjoyed "adequate rest the night before the mission was launched", Robinson taking sedatives to aid the process, though sleeping close to where the U-2 was being pre-flighted did cause a degree of disturbance. MacArthur shadowed his colleague throughout the build-up, ready to step in at any point, something that proved "psychologically encouraging to the primary pilot". An hour before take-off, his mount still inside the hangar, Robinson climbed into the cockpit. The U-2C was towed to the end of the active runway prior to being powered up, finally clearing condensation which had built up on the face plate in the pilot's K-1 high-altitude helmet.

At 09.00 local on 6 December, Robinson and his U-2 got airborne

66 *Not far south of Kuybyshev, he turned the U-2 south-west* 99

from Peshawar and headed north-west. "The initial stage", he wrote, "involved flight over 700 miles of undercast". Climbing through 55,000ft, the tell-tale contrails ceased, only to re-emerge in colder temperatures once the aircraft was established at its 70,000ft operating altitude. "[A] climb was started, to try and clear the contrail layer". This took the U-2 to 73,000ft, where it remained until warmer air permitted a descent back to 70,000.

Robinson had elected to take with him a lethal pill, for use in case of the direst emergency resulting in his being captured on hostile territory. However, he said it was "too dangerous and fragile to carry on an aircraft without special safeguards. The device is also too large to conceal on the person, so it was not in fact carried". He recommended that, "More practical lethal pills be made available to mission pilots."

Navigation on the first leg was performed purely by way of dead-reckoning. "The celestial was only of use for checking ground speeds and there were no radio aids. A forty mile track error resulted on this leg over the undercast, which was corrected 100 miles prior to point E". That particular waypoint was somewhere in the region of Chapayevsk, by which point the Hycon B and Perkin-Elmer tracker cameras were already in operation.

In Robinson's words, "The flight was relatively uneventful", though there was a need to execute one contingency plan. "Due to strong headwinds, two cutoff points were given along the route to reduce the flight plan time in the event of fuel shortage. The first cutoff point was used as the fuel was 30 gallons below the amount required at this point to complete the route… The fact that a higher and less economical profile was being flown at the time also influenced the decision."

At point F, not far south of Kuybyshev — now Samara — he turned the U-2 south-west instead of proceeding further north. As a result, the mission omitted the aircraft plant at Kazan, one of

LEFT:
U-2A 56-6682 served with all three CIA detachments prior to the changes wrought by the Gary Powers shoot-down. This mid-1960s shot shows it as a U-2C.
USAF

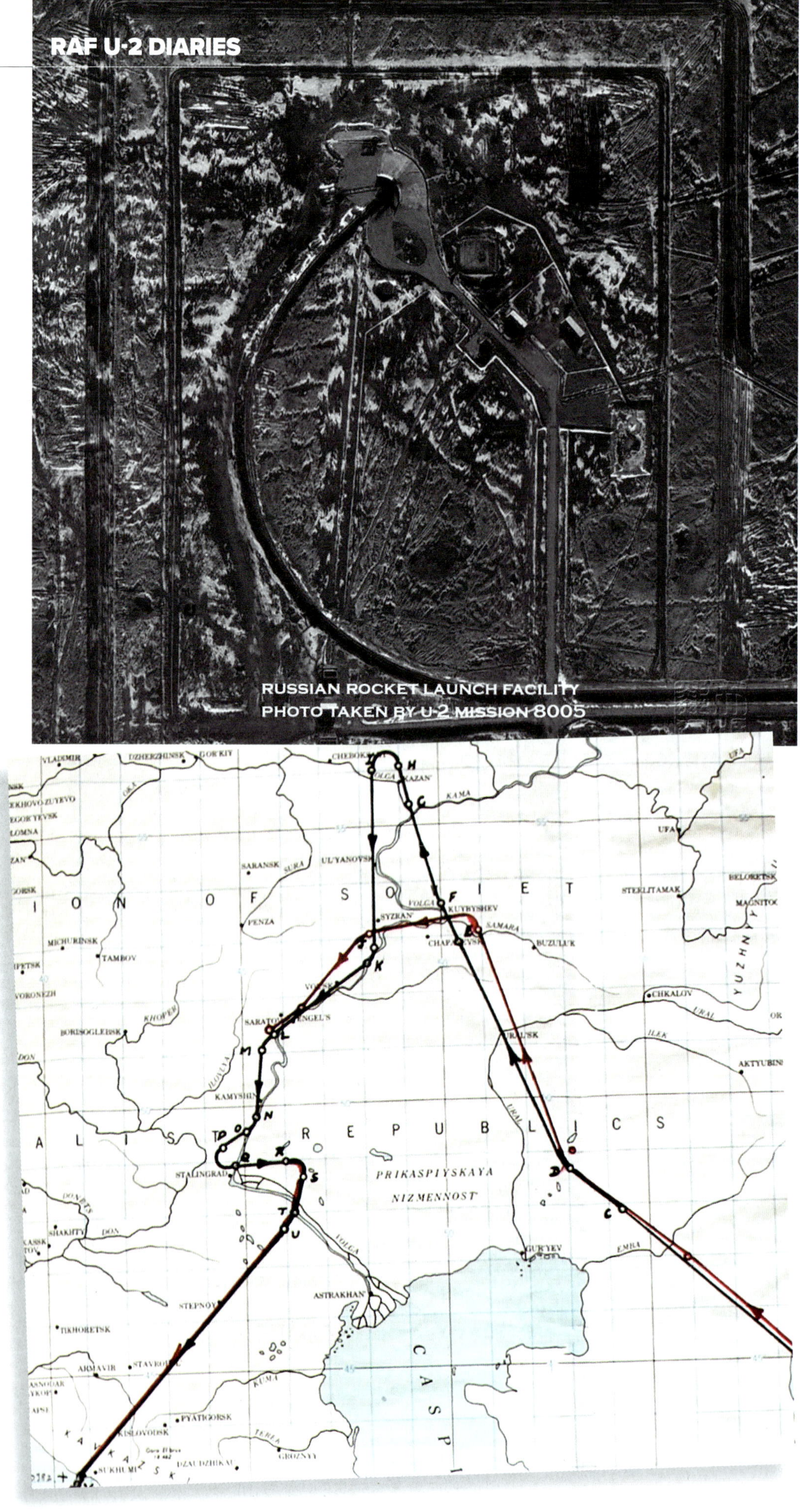

TOP: During his 'High Wire' sortie, Sqn Ldr Robbie Robinson captured the Kapustin Yar ballistic missile test site. NATIONAL ARCHIVES AND RECORDS ADMINISTRATION VIA LIN XU

ABOVE: The main portion of the first RAF-flown U-2 overflight of the Soviet Union, Operation 'High Wire', on 6 December 1959. NATIONAL ARCHIVES

the main centres of Soviet strategic bomber manufacturing. Not far south-west of Syzran, Robinson crossed the track of the longer route and headed back towards it, the two converging near Engels and Saratov.

But the sortie was far from unproductive. In fact, its results were remarkable. Particularly important was Robinson's coverage of the missile test site at Kapustin Yar, which he passed on his way south. To take this in, north of Stalingrad the route bent further west before heading due east, resuming a south-westerly course once past the facility. Only once before had imagery of Kapustin Yar been captured, by a U-2 in the hands of another Detachment B pilot, Bill Hall, on 10 September 1957. 'High Wire' revealed considerable expansion to its surface-to-air missile launch complex, including one completely new launch area, while the surface-to-surface missile facilities now included a further launch complex and enlargement of those seen previously. Overall, said a CIA report, "the number of ballistic and cruise missile launch points has doubled since September 1957."

❖

The weather over the target areas having largely been good, an undercast returned for the final 1,000 miles home. Robinson landed back at Adana after eight-and-a-quarter hours in the air. His efforts had captured not only crucial new details of Kapustin Yar, but also 16 new SAM sites in the areas of Kuybyshev, Saratov and Stalingrad, "a major chemical warfare proving ground" and a hitherto unknown nuclear weapon storage location, to cite but a few. Coverage was obtained of 31 airfields, three of them described as "major new fields", and 1,243 aircraft. Add to these countless other military and industrial facilities, transport and communication links, and much more besides, no wonder one CIA official said 'High Wire' had covered, "probably the highest density of high priority targets in the Soviet Union of any project mission."

In looking back on the year's accomplishments, the first USSR overflight naturally featured highly, Robinson praising "the complete Anglo-American unanimity displayed throughout". Even so, there was some satisfaction to be gained in data showing how the British 'Oldster' pilots had covered more ground on operational missions with the B camera operating, 27,224nm as opposed to 26,156nm, than their American counterparts.

January 1960

On 4 January, wrote Robinson, "we were informed that the Prime Minister had given approval for a further overflight of Russia by a British pilot". This was to be Operation 'Knife Edge'. But although "all possible preparations for the successful accomplishment of this mission were made", unsuitable weather over the target area precluded it from being flown at this stage.

No such problems interfered with ELINT activity. The Soviets having announced plans to fire missiles into an area of the Pacific around 7,000 miles from Tyuratam, beginning on 15 January, Detachment B prepared for additional System VII sorties using the three U-2Cs it now had with the capability.

"Our ability to fly an ELINT flight to coincide with the firing of a missile naturally depends on our obtaining adequate warning of the launch time", reported Robinson. "The minimum warning time needed is four hours and forty-five minutes. Two hours to pre-breathe the pilot [which involved inhaling pure oxygen to remove nitrogen from the bloodstream and prevent decompression sickness] and two and three quarter hours to reach the control point. In previous Russian programmes the pattern of information we have had available has ensured the necessary warning time. When the first missile in this new series was fired, the Russians had altered their count-down procedure and the first indications of a launch attempt were reaching us approximately three hours prior to control time. This precluded any possibility of our pre-breathing a pilot and getting an aircraft into position in time, and it appeared initially as if this series of shots would be missed."

Studying the pattern of operations, however, showed that the first countdown was "almost always a practice", and that following an initial practice, "a launch attempt is invariably made within 72 hours or another practice follows". A new procedure for U-2 missions saw the

A DAY IN THE LIFE...

In January 1959, Sqn Ldr Robbie Robinson sent to London a detailed run-down of how Detachment B prepared for an operational — 'headquarters-directed' — U-2 sortie out of Adana, and the subsequent recovery. Partially reproduced here in edited form, it opens another window onto life within the CIA unit.

PRE-FLIGHT BRIEFING

"For an 08.00hrs take-off, pilot briefing is at 05.15hrs. This necessitates rising at approximately 04.15hrs and cooking one's own breakfast as there are no messing facilities at this time of day. Usually Dr Clifford [the RAF's dedicated 'Oldster' flight surgeon] takes care of the pilot concerned and elects to cook breakfast. He is possibly concerned that we poison ourselves at the present state of the cooking art.

"At the formal pre-flight briefing the pilot is given his route, weather, intelligence, escape and evasion and special equipment operation. Normally only people directly concerned with the flight will be present. Colonel Beerli and myself sit in on all briefings and debriefings of our pilots.

"After briefing the pilot dresses and commences oxygen pre-breathing two hours before scheduled take-off (06.00hrs local). During this time 'on the hose' any final briefings may be given and the pilot has a chance to study his route and flight plan and any relevant intelligence and E&E [electrical and environmental] material. He may however just relax and read gems of American literature such as *Playboy*, *Confessions*, *Gent*, etc!"

GO/NO GO MESSAGE

"The navigators who did initial flight planning the evening before and finished, say, at 01.00hrs will be up before 05.00hrs to complete the flight plan. The winds forecast on the message will have to be applied.

"If any alteration to the flight plan arrives within a few hours of take-off it can cause consternation among the navigators and is a situation which should be avoided if possible. Any late alterations lead to a rush with the associated risk of error."

AIRCRAFT LAUNCHING

"The pilot completes his suiting-up and his pressure equipment is tested, and he is taken out

to the aircraft 30 minutes before take-off. The appendages of survival are hung upon him and he is strapped into the aircraft. After further check of the pressure suit by PE [personal equipment] personnel and Dr Clifford the pilot completes his cockpit check and is ready for start-up. The engine is started eight minutes before take-off and after taxi clearance is obtained the aircraft moves onto the runway three minutes before take-off time. Groundcrew then remove the pogo release pins and the camera hatch covers and signal to the pilot that the aircraft is clear to go.

"After take-off no verbal R/T messages are given. On a discreet frequency the pilot signifies by a series of transmitter clicks that he is proceeding with the flight either fully serviceable, partially unserviceable, or that he is aborting.

"From take-off plus fifteen minutes until landing time minus thirty minutes the listening watch on the discreet frequency is closed down. No contact is expected with the aircraft unless he returns early and calls in on the normal tower control frequencies or on guard channel."

AIRCRAFT RECOVERY

"On return the aircraft R/T messages to the tower are monitored by a detachment mobile controller, who also observes the landing. After landing the pilot taxis clear of the runway where he is met by servicing personnel who reinstall the pogos and replace the camera hatch covers. The aircraft then taxis back to the hangar area.

"The pilot is driven from the aircraft to the PE section by ambulance where he undresses and immediately takes a shower. Scotch, bourbon, beer or soft drinks are available to the pilot according to his wishes. After several hours without liquid the beer is the usual choice."

DEBRIEFING

"A formal debrief of the flight takes place 30 minutes after landing. All maintenance, special equipment, navigation and met personnel directly involved are present. Each person in turn debriefs the pilot on their particular aspect of the flight, and the performance of their equipment. The entire debrief is recorded on tape which is dispatched to HQ."

aircraft taking off "[if] indications of a count-down were received", accepting that the sortie would be unproductive if it turned out to be a practice. This happened twice to Detachment B pilots, before Robinson got airborne on 31 January and picked up indications of an actual firing.

February 1960

Conditions having improved, on 5 February the postponed 'Knife Edge' mission went ahead. It followed the now well-honed deployment procedure for a launch out of Peshawar, albeit with a delay of more than 24 hours caused ➤

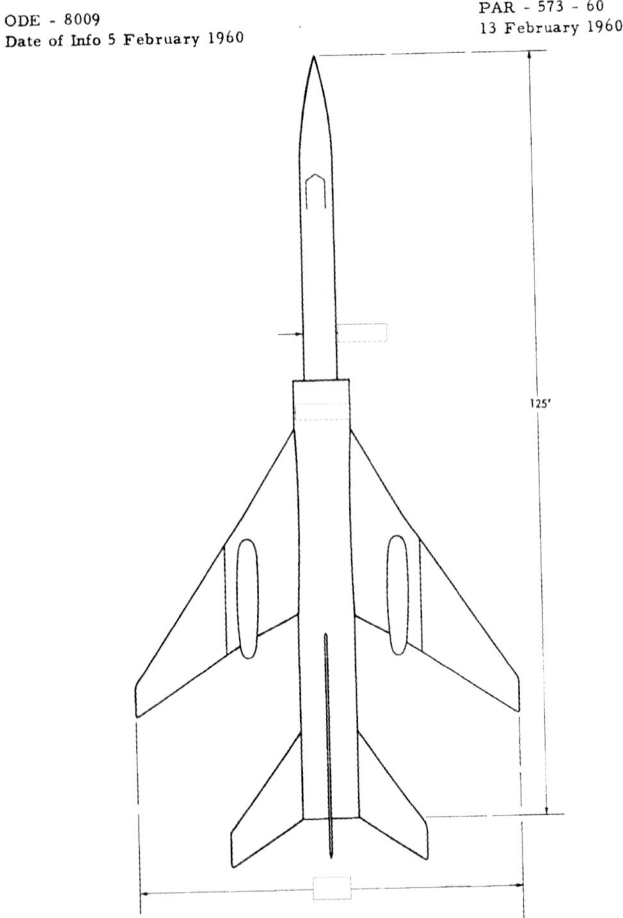

TOP: The image from Operation 'Knife Edge', flown by Flt Lt John MacArthur on 5 February 1960, that gave the west its first glimpse of the Tupolev Tu-22 — subsequently assigned the NATO reporting name 'Blinder'. The six aircraft on the left of this photo of a snow-covered Kazan North airfield are all brand-new Tu-22s, with a seventh parked elsewhere.
NATIONAL ARCHIVES AND RECORDS ADMINISTRATION VIA LIN XU

ABOVE: The drawing of the Tu-22 that resulted from the Kazan North overflight. CIA

by technical problems with the assigned Article 360 — each U-2 was referred to by an Article number — and the need to substitute a different airframe. John MacArthur was the pilot, bound largely for areas of the USSR not previously covered.

Much of the ground was covered in snow as he passed overhead at 65,000ft, to quote a CIA summary, "swinging in a wide arc from the Aral Sea to the Crimea", gathering photographic coverage of "many major items of intelligence interest". These included 18 additional SAM sites and four SAM support installations, two new-type radar installations, and 93 airfields with 1,973 aeroplanes visible on them, among them three hitherto unseen major bases.

One of the existing airfields brought the greatest intelligence coup. Having been omitted from the 6 December sortie, Kazan North was an important objective this time, being the location of State Aircraft Plant No 22. It did not disappoint. Clearly captured outside in the snow by the U-2's cameras were seven examples of a new type, described by the CIA as, "a twin-jet, swept wing bomber with a span of approximately 78 feet and a fuselage length of 125 feet. The wings are cranked approximately one-third of the way out from the fuselage… With the exception of the dimensions being 20 to 25 percent larger, and a few design modifications the airplane resembles Backfin". That was the NATO reporting name for Tupolev's Tu-98 bomber, as shown at the 1956 Tushino display, a single prototype of which had flown.

What MacArthur's cameras had picked up were early specimens of another Tupolev product, the supersonic Tu-22, first flown in prototype form at Zhukovsky the previous August. It had not been seen before by western eyes. Subsequently dubbed 'Blinder', a first series production Tu-22B took to the air from Kazan seven months after the U-2 overflight, in September 1960. Again, with this scoop, 'Oldster' had proved its worth.

─── **March 1960** ───

In "one of the quietest months for Oldster activity since our arrival", Robinson noted how there had been no operational activity. However, there was flying to be done, for the U-2Cs were newly fitted with slipper tanks, which required testing on simulated mission profiles. "The increase in range was as calculated and no adverse handling characteristics resulted", said the detachment commander.

With March's offering, the 'Oldster' dispatches come to an end. It seems doubtful that a report for April exists, given the circumstances in which the Adana detachment suddenly had to close. Back in London, Macmillan was starting to get cold feet. Despite the lack of any Soviet response to the two overflights by British pilots, he and others in government were becoming twitchy about creating an international incident. After all, at best, the sorties were

on shaky legal ground. And the Soviets were aware. Following the 5 February U-2 mission, the British high commissioner in Karachi reported back to London that they were putting pressure on Pakistan regarding the use of its facilities by British forces.

These concerns were soon born out. While the PM wavered, Eisenhower wanted still more intelligence on Moscow's ballistic missile programmes. He authorised another overflight, 'Square Deal', for 9 April. This had been planned in large part by the 'Oldster' team, but was flown by an American, Bob Ericson. It covered such objectives as the Sary Shagan anti-missile testing range, the Semipalatinsk nuclear test site and, once again, Tyuratam. As an annotated map in the 'Oldster' files shows, flying south towards Zahedan, Iran, where the U-2 was to land, Ericson detected a possible Soviet fighter response. In fact, the USSR's air defence force, the PVO, had tracked the aircraft almost since it passed into Soviet territory, scrambling MiG-19 and new Su-9 interceptors. Yet this did not prevent approval of Operation 'Grand Slam', the 1 May overflight across the USSR from south-east to north-west. The resulting shoot-down of Article 360 and its pilot Gary Powers by an SA-2 SAM could, perhaps, have been predicted.

Cue a scramble to remove the British element from Detachment B, the pilot cadre being flown out of Adana by what the CIA called "a 'black' airlift" and returned to London for debriefing. The agency's U-2 detachments, meanwhile, were withdrawn from their overseas locations. Operations would henceforth be concentrated at the Edwards AFB North Base in California, and RAF pilots were part of them. That was the case right up until the CIA ceased flying the aircraft in 1974. But, through an abundance of political caution, none of them ever flew an operational U-2 reconnaissance mission. That honour belonged solely to the 'Oldster' contingent.

With thanks to Chris Pocock.

MEIER MOTORS

The team behind the German warbird restoration shop with a host of outstanding, and rare, projects to its credit

WORDS: BEN DUNNELL

The core Meier Motors team at Bremgarten this spring: from left to right, Elmar and Achim Meier, and co-CEOs Marc Lais and Julian Heinrich. VIA MEIER MOTORS

Adolf Meier's immaculate MS500 Criquet at Freiburg airfield in 1978.
LANDESARCHIV BADEN-WÜRTTEMBERG

Today's warbird scene is, it need hardly be said, a very different affair compared with even a couple of decades ago. Many of the famous, established operators are still around and going strong. But they've been joined by an array of new entrants, all with particular motivations driving their interest. Some maintain a straightforward, old-style passion for these aircraft and flying them. Others, starting out with little or no prior experience, may hope to develop such an enthusiasm. There are those who view their purchases as more of an investment, or see revenue-generating opportunities for them. Equally, they may wish just to enjoy them privately. Whatever the category, historic aeroplanes have — to use a cliché — become big business, and from that has stemmed a professional, commercial industry dedicated to maintaining, restoring and operating them. This is one reason why Meier Motors, based at Bremgarten in south-western Germany, has flourished. The company counts among its

clients some of the world's leading collections, as well as owners with just a single aeroplane, and its output speaks for itself.

The name is now known on the entire warbird scene, but it stems, as these things often do, from small beginnings. Achim and Elmar Meier started out with no grand intentions, but the brothers' interests in flying and engineering formed a firm basis on which to build. Meier Motors now occupies its own immaculate premises at Bremgarten airfield, filling multiple hangars, and employs in the region of 20 people. Achim and Elmar are still heavily involved, but in 2022 the reins were handed over to long-time team members Marc Lais and Julian Heinrich, who are now the firm's joint chief executives. They joined Achim for our interview, in the bar next to the hangar complex.

Achim and Elmar's late father Adolf was a farmer. "He had a disability", says Achim, "because one day he was riding a motorcycle to Freiburg with his elder brother and they had an accident, colliding ●

Two of the Mustangs to have passed through the Meier Motors facilities. Nearest is TF-51D D-FTSI, for a long time owned by Maxi Gainza, but later sold to a new owner and repainted as *Double Trouble Two*; it was sold to the USA in 2021. P-51D N4034S *Miss Stress*, behind it, is still at Bremgarten. UWE GLASER

The first Yak-3 worked on by the Meiers was D-FJAK, pictured during 2003 with Achim at the controls. DR ANDREAS ZEITLER

with oncoming traffic. My uncle was killed, and my father lost his left arm. His interest in farming was the technical side, and he went to a French auction at Freiburg airfield to buy Unimogs. But the whole lot was bought by a Swedish guy. There was this poor old aeroplane sitting there with its wings folded. The engine had the pistons and cylinders off, and pushrods hanging out of it. He was going to buy this shit!"

The aircraft in question was an Argus-engined Morane-Saulnier MS500 Criquet, a French licence-built Fieseler Fi 156 Storch, registered D-EAML. "We already had one Unimog, so he drove it there and towed the aircraft by road to our farm. He put it in the back garden, because the farm buildings were too small for it. Eventually he had to extend the shed to get it all in, and then he started in his spare time to restore it. Because he only had one arm, he always needed help. My brother and I also spent most of our spare time in that shed, holding stuff for him and doing things. We had no understanding at that time.

"Finally in 1972 it was finished. There was already a Storch in Freiburg, and he asked the owner and pilot if he would do the test-

flying. They did the licensing, the paperwork and everything, and that guy flew it. He paid my father a lot of compliments, that it flew very nicely, the engine worked perfectly and everything was great. So, my father decided to get his pilot's licence. He started off, but again it was difficult because of being one-armed. They decided he had to do his licence flying from the right-hand seat, as

> **The Yak-11 was the big start, without us really knowing it**

he only had his right arm. He was able to do it, and he had special entries on his licence. It was very complicated, so it was a long time before he was able to fly the Storch.

"He started taking it to airshows, and I was always with him. I think by the time I was 10 or 12 I had more hours in it than I flew during my regular PPL training! By the time I could actually get my licence, I was

pissed-off with everything I had to do... Elmar was the same. Aged 15, he overhauled an Argus engine with our father at home on the farm. He had the technical brain; I wasn't even interested in that. Some time afterwards, we rebuilt a Toyota Land Cruiser. We were outside, it was beautiful weather, we looked up and there was a Cessna flying over. We said, 'Hey, what about flying? Shall we get our licences?' Both of us went to the flying school in Freiburg, the Flugschule Harter, signed up and started flying again.

"My brother was working for Mercedes, but he moved to the flying school and started getting his aviation mechanic licences. Later on he became a licensed airframe inspector. I did the flying side — I got my instrument rating, instructor's rating, CPL [commercial pilot licence]. But you couldn't get your ATPL [airline transport pilot licence] in Freiburg then, and some friends of mine went off to get that in Frankfurt. They asked me if I'd like to join them, but Elmar said, 'Hey Achim, then everything would stop.'"

He was referring to their burgeoning involvement with old aircraft. In 1990 they acquired their own Piper Super Cub, and soon they

were flying the MS500. After that, says Achim, "We bought a former crop-sprayer Stearman from Rob Simpson in Gloucester, a horrible thing, and we were able to use the workshop in the flying school to restore it in our spare time. I decided maybe he was right, and I said I'd stay. Then Mr Harter said if I stayed I could become his main flying instructor. The only interesting aircraft they had was a Piper Navajo, and I was able to fly that."

The Stearman gave way in 1996 to a Harvard IV, purchased from Tony Haig-Thomas at North Weald. "I was so impressed with Tony himself, in his proper flying suit. Tony is so British. He's great. I remember he wore the same cord trousers every day, and after a few days I was wondering whether he had another pair. We flew in the aircraft, and I told him we'd dreamed of this aeroplane and we really wanted to buy it, but our budget was limited. I gave him an envelope with the money in it. We were eating, and he opened the envelope and looked inside it. His face went more and more red, and he put the envelope down. We were sitting there and we couldn't eat — we were looking at him. What the hell was going on, what will he say?

I asked, 'Will we continue flying, or shall we go back home?' He said, 'Never do this again…' We had a deal.

———————— ❖ ————————

"Then we bought a Yak-11 from someone in Le Castellet. That one, actually, was our favourite. It was a great aeroplane. But our main shareholder was a former Phantom pilot, and I made one mistake — I took him in the Yak-11. You know, the engine shakes; it's a seven-cylinder direct-injection engine, so it's never going to be smooth like a T-6. After landing,

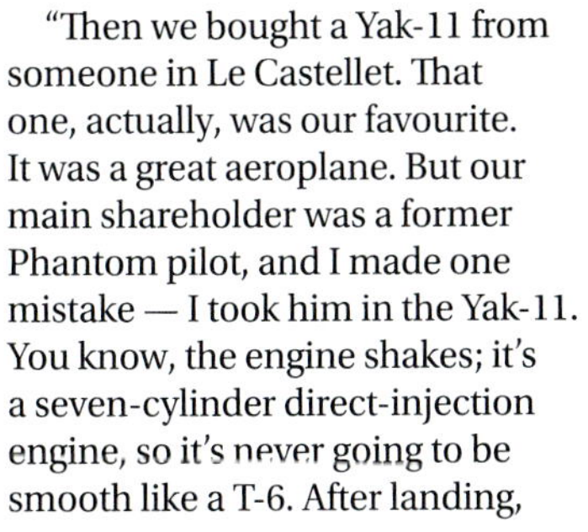

he said, 'You know, Achim, I never liked the MiG-29… I like American aeroplanes. So, please do me one favour. Can you sell this aeroplane as soon as possible?' So, we had to sell it, but we did a fantastic deal with Egidio Gavazzi. The outcome was great.

"Egidio had told me about a dear friend at North Weald who had a Yak-11, and he needed to have a nicer one — they had a bit of a competition going on… It was a nice Yak-11, it was a beauty. We flew together for 10 minutes and he said, 'Wow, this is the perfect aeroplane. We will buy it.' He asked me to bring it up to North Weald, and that was the first time I met Maxi Gainza. I landed, and there was Egidio, completely proud. Maxi said hello, and then, 'Yes, you're right. This is much nicer than mine.' Egidio had a big grin…

"The Yak was the big start, without us really knowing it. We were thinking about what we could go for after a Yak-11. A Mustang was a dream, but we didn't have the money. Then on 11 September 2001 I was at Reno. We were sitting around, because every day the guys promised they'd be able to fly, and we realised after a few days they wouldn't. In *Trade-A-Plane* there was an advertisement from Bob Hannah for a Yak-3, so I checked how far it was to Idaho. There was a guy from Freiburg there, a private pilot, and we were talking about what to do. I said we could look at the Yak-3, and he told me, 'Hey, I have this huge Cadillac. I have time — that would be great.' So, we drove up to Boise and met Bob Hannah. Fantastic guy.

"We looked at the aeroplane… it was very nice, very clean, but I thought we wouldn't be able to do anything with the price. The other guy was making promises: 'Yeah, ⟶

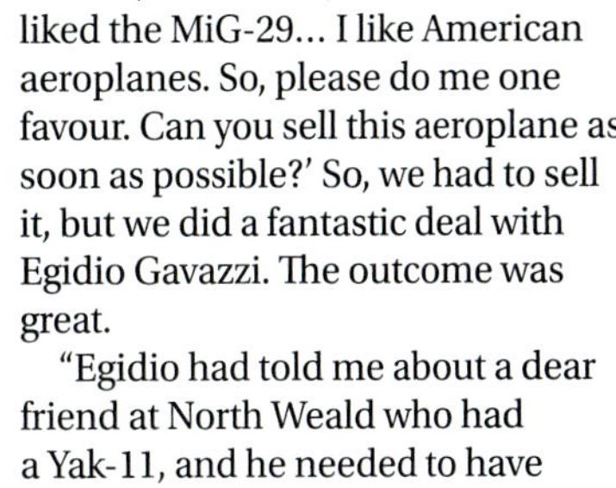

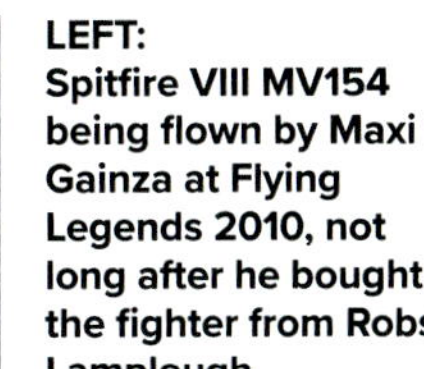

BELOW LEFT:
The first Flug Werk
FW 190 A-8/N
to receive Meier
Motors' attention
was D-FMFW for
Jerry Yagen. He later
sold this example,
but bought another.
K.-L. MÜLLER

LEFT:
Getting ready for the
Yak four-ship at ILA
2006 in Berlin, Elmar
Meier (second from
right) talks to British
pilot Clive Davidson.
DR ANDREAS ZEITLER

ABOVE:
P-51D D-FPSI, the second Mustang put onto the German register at Meier Motors, received Swiss Air Force colours for 2014's centenary of that air arm. Then owned by Christoph Nöthiger, it has subsequently changed hands and is still resident.
RICHARD PAVER

yeah, we'll come back and buy it'. I was keeping very calm. We flew back home, and I spoke to my brother. He said, 'Let's go to the Volksbank and see what they say'. But there was still this other guy from Freiburg who'd said we should buy it and share it. I called him and said I'd had a call from Bob Hannah and we'd promised to buy the aeroplane. What was the latest from his side? He told me the stock market was going badly and he couldn't do it, so he was out. So, we went to the bank and my brother somehow got a deal. The bank would finance us buying the Yak-3.

"The aircraft went into a container and was shipped. It came to Freiburg and we looked at everything. My brother also didn't really like the Russian style of construction, because they had to make so many compromises. After a year we'd taken it apart and put it back together a couple of times, and we learned a lot, like how the oil tank was made of 0.3mm aluminium and glued, not welded. There were some accidents I read stories about as well. We rebuilt everything; we put a nice stainless-steel oil tank in, we used proper materials, we modified the engine mount. I think in the end we made 17 modifications to the Yak-3 before I went up in the aeroplane. But then I had fun!

"Egidio Gavazzi had moved from London to St Moritz, and to clear customs he always went via Freiburg. He would pay us a visit [...] and he was always amazed with the Yak-3. He said his friend Maxi Gainza had a Yak-3 [...] and he was very disappointed. There was no progress, and it was sitting somewhere in Lithuania. I told Egidio that Maxi should call me any time and we would give him advice. It took three or four months, but then Maxi called. He wanted me to join him for an inspection of the Yak-3 so he knew where he was with it. We agreed, and we met in Vilnius and went up to the place... the first thing we saw was that the gear had not extended fully and could fold up. I said, 'Maxi, there's a problem',

> ## " We went to the bank and got them to finance half of the Mustang "

and so it started. It was a 'home run' for us, with all our experience of the Yak-3... Three months later, he called and said he wanted the aeroplane to be shipped to our place.

"Maxi's aircraft we did in the flying school hangar. We promised we would finish it on my brother's birthday, 22 October 2004. It was ready to fly, but we were missing the paperwork from the LBA [Luftfahrtbundesamt, the German CAA], so we told Maxi as a surprise that he could fly our Yak instead. He was thrilled by this offer, so he took off. Freiburg's runway then was

1,000m long, but it was restricted by buildings and trees, so he didn't want to land there. He landed here at Bremgarten instead. I flew over and brought the aircraft back. Maxi was thrilled, and when his aeroplane flew it was a star. We wondered whether it was a perfect operation in Freiburg with the short runway. If I'd been a customer, I'd have taken my aircraft somewhere else. That was something we had in mind. After Maxi's aeroplane, it happened so quickly. We had eight Yak-3s and Yak-9s imported into Germany."

A major highlight was the ILA 2006 airshow in Berlin, where the Meiers displayed three Yak-3s and an R-2000-engined Yak-11. One of them was the Yak-3 owned by Jerry Yagen, newly brought back to flying condition after suffering a ground-loop with its previous owner in South Africa. He then contracted Achim and Elmar to get his Flug Werk FW 190 A-8/N airworthy, and to take on a Messerschmitt Bf 109 G project using an HA-1112-M1L Buchón airframe and the remains of a Bf 109 G-4, Werknummer 19257, recovered from Russia. These were among the aircraft at Freiburg when, in October 2006, the brothers started their own company. Another client at the time was Chris Vogelgesang, who ended up obtaining their first Yak-3. He suggested the name Meier Motors.

Achim looked at buying the ex-David Gilmour P-51D Mustang with Chris, but they missed out. However, it wasn't long before an initial pair of P-51s arrived with Meier Motors to be put on the German register. The second was acquired from the Real Aeroplane Company after Elmar met 'Taff' Smith at Duxford during the 2007 Flying Legends show. "He called and said there was a Mustang for sale not far away. Could he get it? I said, 'A Mustang? We've no money!' Always the same story, isn't it? But he went to Breighton, and 'Taff' Smith said he'd put a ferry tank in because he wanted to fly it to Oshkosh and sell it there. So, Elmar said, 'We'll buy the aeroplane'. He came back home and said, 'I shook hands to buy that Mustang'. I went, 'Are you crazy?' We went to the bank again, and got them to finance 50 per cent of it. For the other 50 per cent, it was, 'Maxi, we need to have dinner and a nice bottle of wine...'" Meier Motors has since sold that same Mustang twice more.

The move to Bremgarten in 2008 was conducted in partnership with

Maxi Gainza. He set up MaxAlpha Aviation to run his fleet, managed by Achim. "The first aeroplane in the new hangar was his Yak, and he said, 'Achim, will we ever fill up this place?' I think it was two years later when we ran out of space". A stream of new arrivals saw to that, not least an F4U-5NL Corsair, Spitfire VIII MV154 and a TF-51D Mustang, all for Maxi himself. There was Spitfire XVI TE184 for Stephen Stead, who was an existing customer through a Yak-3. There were still more Mustangs. And there were many projects for the late Volker Schülke's Hangar 10/Air Fighter Academy operation at Heringsdorf, to name but a few.

Aside from the company's own team, Achim credits three people for their roles in Meier Motors' success. Maxi, naturally, is one; Jerry Yagen another. The third is the late Dieter Thomas, the former Dornier chief test pilot, whose consultancy was of enormous assistance in getting LBA approval for many warbird projects. It's all provided a firm foundation on which to build, and for the new CEOs to take over.

❖

Both Marc Lais and Julian Heinrich have been with Meier Motors since the 2000s, starting on the maintenance side before moving on to restorations and other broader responsibilities. Thus, they've seen how things have grown and developed, helping formulate their own takes on the future. But what of the present? A walk through the hangars revealed a striking array of types, mainly historic. Work on modern general aviation machines is a useful income source, and a way for the staff to gain extra engineering

licences. The focus, though, is still absolutely on classics.

As of now, about eight different P-51Ds have come through Meier Motors, and three — N4034S *Miss Stress*, D-FPSI *See Me Later* and Georg Raab's NL51ZW *Frances Dell* — were on hand during our visit. Spitfires have been no strangers either, and MkXVIII SM845, so familiar on the UK circuit when owned by Richard Lake, was under maintenance. It was purchased by the same owner as *Miss Stress.* Another MkXVIII, TP280, was brought in by road from the Hangar 10 facility at Heringsdorf, having not been flown for a couple of years. This machine needed to be recertified prior to shipment to Peter Timmermans in Canada.

A growing specialism in Sea Furies had already seen Bristol Centaurus-powered ex-Iraqi Fury ISS D-CRZY being prepared and delivered to Stefano Landi in Italy, while a pair of two-seat T20s were in the workshop. N1954H has a Wright R-3350 engine, the intention being to sell it as a practical aircraft for an owner to enjoy, as its previous custodian did, flying it both VFR and IFR. As part of this, Meier Motors is fitting a second oil radiator to reduce the risk of overheating on the ground, in a similar configuration to the Corsair. D-CACE, in its original scarlet colours as an ex-Deutscher Luftfahrt-Beratungsdienst target-tug, is equipped with a Centaurus. The milestone of a first engine run was achieved this September.

Having been converted to its present configuration by Meier Motors for Hangar 10, the Messerschmitt Stiftung's two-seat Bf 109 G-12 was in for regular maintenance. Buchón C.4K-187, formerly G-AWHM with Air Leasing, was ready to fly with a new German owner. An exceptional presence, meanwhile, was Bf 109 E-3a Werknummer 2372 from the Hangar 10 stable. This restoration of an aircraft that crashed in Austria during November 1940 has progressed a long way.

"Our customers don't want a new aircraft, of course", says Marc Lais. "They want a unique piece of history. But we need to find a good balance between a safe, flying aircraft and that piece of history. It's not easy to decide whether to keep a certain part because it belongs to the aircraft if it's going to be airworthy. This is ➧

ABOVE:
Italian owner Stefano Landi's Fury ISS D-CRZY was reflown in September 2020.
LUIGINO CALIARO

why projects like these take so many years. Yes, they're small aircraft with only a handful of systems, but each system is special, and you have to do a lot of research and engineering.

"We work together with the Messerschmitt Stiftung, as they have a lot of experience operating these engines — the DB605 especially. Another good thing is that the engine in Jerry Yagen's G-4 proves that the technology and the maintenance schedule can work in operation."

While plenty of familiarity with Flug Werk's FW 190 A-8/Ns has been amassed — Meier Motors completed Jerry Yagen's first example, and a second for a German owner — the 'long-nose' FW 190 D-9/N model is another matter. The airframe being worked on is a further member of Yagen's collection, acquired from Kissimmee, Florida-based Tom Blair. "The project was a kind of a 'hangar queen'", Marc Lais recalls. "In the past an Allison [V-1710] engine was installed. Years later Achim told me about this project and that Jerry Yagen wanted to make it airworthy, but he had a special idea: they wanted to install everything in accordance with the original manufacturing. This, of course, means the Jumo engine and the correct propeller.

"He wanted us to bring all the modifications we've made to the

A-models in the past into this aeroplane — and we made a lot of modifications. We also modified the electric motors for the gear retraction mechanism. We have rebuilt the

---

> ## ❝ *We need aircraft to help give people a start* ❞

---

wing, because we know the wing structure needs to be modified; we have that experience from flight-testing our last [A-8/N] project. It needs to be strengthened, especially on the lower main spar position. From the firewall to the rudder is

also 75 per cent complete. The key is to get the engine done — the correct engine mounts, the cooling system — and that's a challenge. Everything is in progress, but it's not here in our shop. Mike Nixon [of Vintage V-12s in California] has done the engine, and Skycraft [in Royston, Hertfordshire] has done the propeller."

Still we were far from finished. The FM-2 Wildcat owned by B&B Old Aviation was under repair, its sturdiness apparent from the relatively minor damage it suffered in a nose-over. Nearby, the MaxAlpha Corsair was undergoing its annual. Fiat G59-4B D-FIAT was an exquisite vision in polished silver. Assorted Harvards, T-28s and other trainers were no less pristine, to say nothing of a Beech 18 from the Swiss Classic Formation, in for

RIGHT:
An absolutely stunning project has been Merlin-engined EKW C-3603 D-FEKW for a private owner, which Swiss Air Force pilot Lukas Meier — no relation — took into the air at Bremgarten on 4 June 2021.
MATTHIAS DORST

maintenance. Clearly, the client base remains very strong. What's the management's perspective?

"Our customers are getting older", says Marc Lais, "and while we have really good customers, we don't have hundreds of them. It's a small circle of enthusiasts". How, then, can that circle be expanded? "We need aircraft to help give people a start. In mainland Europe, and in Germany in particular, it's not easy to get a licence. I think that's the biggest step involved in getting people in and making them more interested in vintage aircraft. Basically, a lot of people are interested in vintage aviation but they think it's impossible to get into it."

One current client shows how it can be done. Having never previously gone so far as to dream of having his own Mustang, not only does he own one — *Miss Stress* — but he flies it and several other warbirds himself, having used a TF-51D for training. "I think it's necessary for a company to have training aircraft, just to catch the people, to give them an idea of what it means to be a warbird pilot."

Julian Heinrich adds, "We would like to offer a package, to give people the opportunity to get in touch with these aeroplanes and a way to get their licence while we prepare their aircraft for them. That's what we are mostly focusing on". Another aspect is typified by the Sea Fury radiator modification, the aim to make the aircraft more friendly and practical for their owners. "That's how Meier Motors started with the Yaks", says Marc. "The aircraft were OK, they were working and they were safe, but Achim and Elmar's idea was always to modify them to make them safer and easier to operate. We want to move ahead with that."

That's especially important in Germany, where there's less airshow work to be had than, say, there still is in the UK. Indeed, a lot of the private-owner clients are just that. "Most of them want to operate the aircraft for themselves", Marc states. "I think 75 per cent of our customers are not focused on airshows". Nor is there any formal framework in Germany under which paid warbird passenger rides are allowed. With such familiar concerns as rising avgas prices and airfield operating restrictions much to the fore, owner-pilots need to be sure their aeroplanes will afford them maximum use and enjoyment.

For Achim Meier, involvement with another aircraft has brought a welcome change of emphasis. This is A-26B Invader N500MR, the stunning On Mark-converted example owned by Tina Fly, which he set up in 2018. Meier

Motors undertook a pre-purchase inspection when the aircraft was still based at Tatoi near Athens, but otherwise Tina Fly, run by Martina Paul, is a wholly separate operation. Instead of dealing with customers, Achim says, "I'm the one who says what we'll do on the aeroplane, who's doing what and how far we will go with the restoration. Everything is done exactly how I want it. It opens your eyes."

There are new ways of going about major restorations, and it makes sense for an operation on the scale of Meier Motors to use them. Marc Lais comments, "The key is technology. In the future we would like to have CAD [computer-aided design] and CNC [computer numerical control] technology to fabricate parts. What we do here is craftsmanship, but that's state-of-the-art. The quality is the same, but at the moment it takes time."

Yet whenever — or however — the end product emerges, the sense of anticipation and excitement surrounding the big moment will be as great as it's always been. As Achim Meier puts it, "When you see the quality and you sit in the aircraft, you can't wait to go flying. That's great". So it's been for the dozens of other owners whose aeroplanes have passed through the doors of Meier Motors, and which will continue to do so. **A**

SHUTTLEWOR

The late **Pete Whalley**, a Liverpool-based enthusiast and photographer, took these outstanding colour images at Old Warden on an historic occasion — 14 June 1964, the date of the Shuttleworth Collection's first public air display

Dickie Martin handles the Avro 504K, which carried serial E3404; later this was changed to H5199, the airframe's correct identity.

Looking well-used, Comper Swift G-ABUS was owned at the time by John Sumner Edwards and Peter Devey. Edwards later acquired G-ACTF, the Swift today in Shuttleworth's hands.

DH60 Moth G-EBLV was then owned by Hawker Siddeley, successor to its manufacturer, in whose possession the ADC Cirrus III-engined machine had been since 1941. Only in March of last year was 'LV transferred to Shuttleworth ownership. At the 1964 display it was flown by Desmond Penrose. Behind it is Spitfire PRXI PL983, kept outside at Old Warden for a long time before being sold; it is now with the Aircraft Restoration Company.

TH 1964

Druine D5 Turbi G-AOTK was built at the premises of Hatfield Technical College by de Havilland apprentices, who made up the TK Flying Group, and was proclaimed to be the first British amateur-built aircraft of post-war design. It flew for the first time in August 1958.

A flypast from Currie Wot G-APWT, the second example of the type, back in conventional Walter Mikron piston-engine form after its time as the 'Jet Wot' with a Rover gas turbine. It is extant in the USA, if not presently airworthy.

DH53 Humming Bird G-EBHX and Hawker Tomtit G-AFTA, both part of the collection nearly 60 years later. The Tomtit was still in its Hawker 'house colours', despite having been sold to Shuttleworth in 1960. In those more relaxed days, see how cars and crowds were spread around the entire airfield boundary!

Lightning F1 XM147, in the hands of No 74 Squadron CO Sqn Ldr John Howe, in the near-vertical for *The Aeroplane*'s photographer Alfred Long. He was aboard a Meteor NF14. *AEROPLANE*

THE THOUSAND MILE AN HOUR CLUB

Being part of No 74 Squadron's first operational cadre on the sensational English Electric Lightning F1 brought little in the way of operational flying, but a great deal of satisfaction and enjoyment — not least through display flying in those heady early-1960s days **WORDS:** DENIS J. CALVERT

The CO (right) with some of 74's initial cadre of Lightning pilots on the Coltishall flightline in February 1961. David Jones, interviewed by Denis Calvert for this feature, is fifth from left.
AEROPLANE

ABOVE:
A nice box-four rounds the apex of a loop, the CO up front. *AEROPLANE*

"**W**ant to occupy the single seat in the single-seater, all-weather, night-and-day, high-flying, supersonic, supernormal Lightning? Want to climb two Everests in three minutes?" The lines may grate a bit, but the 1962 Air Ministry film *Streaked Lightning* is great fun. Lasting just short of five minutes and shot in a mix of colour and black-and-white, it contains excellent and dramatic footage of the departure of a No 74 Squadron Lightning F1 taken from the undershoot at Coltishall, high-energy manoeuvring above the clouds and a most impressive night three-ship afterburner take-off. Sixty-one years on, it's well worth five minutes of your time to watch online. It also serves to demonstrate how the English Electric fighter was, beyond the operational capabilities it offered, perhaps the most potent publicity tool the post-war RAF had yet possessed.

The service was late onto the scene in introducing a supersonic jet fighter. The disastrous Defence White Paper of March 1957 put an end to several promising supersonic projects from Britain's aviation industry, leaving only English Electric's Lightning — or P1B, as it was then referred to — to progress to squadron service. The decision to spare the Lightning was influenced by the fact that serious money had been spent on its development and testing, and by a belief that the aircraft might prove useful as an interceptor until missiles took over.

It had been a long time coming. Its origins were in specification F23/49 and the P1A, two examples of which were built, the first flying on 4 August 1954. As a result of unclear requirements and a muddled procurement policy, the RAF missed out of a whole generation of 'Mach 1.3' fighters typified by North American's F-100 Super Sabre and Dassault's Super Mystère B2. Three P1B prototypes and 20 development batch Lightnings followed, but it would be six years before the definitive F1 would be ready to join a front-line squadron.

No 74 'Tiger' Squadron was tasked with introducing the Lightning into RAF service during the summer of 1960. Finally, the RAF had a Mach 2 fighter, even if the initial Controller, Aircraft release restricted it to Mach 1.7. The Lightning F1 was the first production variant and just 20

examples (XM134-147 and XM163-168) were built. No 74 Squadron was destined to be the only front-line user of this mark, before production switched to the improved F1A. Apart from XM168, which was a test airframe and never flew, virtually all the others served at some point with 74. Although the total number of Lightnings produced was relatively low at 339, at least eight different marks would serve with the RAF.

David Jones, who joined the squadron when it was still flying the Hunter, converted to the Lightning and lived through those first, eventful years. He would go on to achieve 838 hours on type, serving with Nos 74 and 19 Squadrons before being posted as an instructor on the Lightning operational conversion unit, No 226 OCU.

"When I was leaving school", says David, "the careers advisor wasn't helpful. He told me the subject I was least bad at was maths, so I should become an accountant. So, I started to train as a chartered accountant, but I didn't find that very exciting, and thought flying aeroplanes might be more fun. I walked into a recruiting office in Cambridge and found that they made me quite welcome. As a result, I stopped training as an accountant and joined the RAF in February 1956.

"I did my basic training at RAF Kirton in Lindsey. Then the group was broken into two parts, with half of us to stay in the UK and half to go to Canada. I was lucky enough to be with those who went to Canada. I left the UK in July 1956, and eventually arrived at the RCAF station at Penhold, Alberta, where they had Harvards. I spent about nine months flying the Harvard and did about 180 hours, dual and solo. Then we moved on to Gimli, Manitoba flying the T-33. I did about 90 hours there and was lucky to end up with a white instrument rating, which most other people didn't achieve.

"Then it was back to the UK and on to Vampires at RAF Worksop, where we had to get used to the idea that, on a good day, you could see about three miles and on a bad day about 1,000 yards, whereas in Canada, on a bad day you could see 50 miles and on a good day about 80 miles. So, it was a big learning curve, but I survived the Vampire course. When we were asked to make our choices, I said I'd like to be a fighter pilot. I was lucky, was put in that

RIGHT:
David Jones was already on No 74 Squadron, flying Hunters, when the Lightning came along in 1960.
DAVID JONES COLLECTION

stream, and went to Chivenor and No 229 OCU to fly the Hunter, which at the time was the Hunter F4. To my amazement, I came out of Chivenor with an 'above average' for air firing, but I think it was a total fluke.

"In summer 1958 I was posted to No 74 Squadron at RAF Horsham St Faith, flying Hunter F6s. Within a matter of weeks, I was in Cyprus with the squadron, to spend 10 weeks at Nicosia. Then we went back to Horsham St Faith and in 1959 we moved to RAF Coltishall."

At that time, Coltishall housed two front-line squadrons: No 23 Squadron with Javelins and No 74 Squadron with Hunters. Also based was the Air Fighting Development Squadron, a part of the Central Fighter Establishment. In December 1959 came the announcement that No 74 Squadron was to be the RAF's first front-line Lightning unit and, on the 23rd, development batch Lightning XG334 arrived at Coltishall for the AFDS.

> ## 66 *It was all rather exciting for us to see this new aeroplane* 99

No 74 Squadron's 'boss' at the time was Sqn Ldr Peter Carr, but he was offered the chance to become project director and reserve driver with Donald Campbell's Bluebird land speed record project and left the RAF. Taking over on 22 February 1960 was Sqn Ldr John Howe, a straight-talking South African.

"In late 1959 and early 1960, Lightnings were appearing at Coltishall from time to time to visit AFDS", says David Jones. "It was all rather exciting for us to see this new aeroplane. On 29 June 1960, the first Lightning F1 [XM165] for No 74 Squadron arrived at Coltishall, and the boss and some of the more senior guys started to fly it [Howe made his first Lightning flight on 11 July]. John Howe soon proved to be very much the man for the job. A very experienced pilot, he was tough and didn't suffer fools gladly, but he was also very sympathetic and a good leader. He led from the front."

The task of converting No 74 Squadron's pilots to the Lightning F1 was undertaken by the AFDS and its offshoot, the Lightning Conversion Unit at Coltishall. This was long before the establishment of No 226 OCU and two years prior to the availability of a two-seat Lightning trainer, the T4. Hunter flying reduced from May 1960 as the first batch of eight pilots — half the squadron — started on their conversion. First was a five-day aviation medicine course at RAF Upwood, followed by ground school and lectures on the Lightning and its systems, before going on to the Lightning simulator for one-hour 'sorties'. New to the pilots was the Taylor helmet, which initially proved unpopular. It was heavier than the cloth helmet worn in the Hunter, it restricted head movement and its centre of gravity was situated further forward.

"Prior to the first solo, we all did 10 trips in the simulator at Coltishall", David Jones states. "'Simulator', though, is quite a generous word. It was a procedure trainer; there was no motion and no vision, although there was a bit of sound. Looking back, it did fly quite well, but before you'd flown the real aeroplane, it was a real handful. You weren't really sure what to expect. And when flying, you get so much feedback through the seat of your pants, something you just didn't get in the simulator. All the instruments

ABOVE:
All three aircraft in this formation carry a pair of dummy DH Firestreak air-to-air missiles, the real thing having been scarce. *AEROPLANE*

ABOVE:
A nine-aircraft practice for 74's contribution to the 1961 Paris Salon.
AEROPLANE

worked, though, and you could go through the emergency procedures, but physically flying the aeroplane — the simulator — accurately was quite difficult until you'd flown the real aeroplane a bit."

Ground school instruction is recalled as being somewhat basic and teaching aids primitive: overhead projectors and blackboards. Pilots attended courses on the Lightning by visiting Rolls-Royce at Derby for the Avon engine and to Ferranti in Edinburgh for the AI Mk23 radar. Despite the squadron expecting delivery of three more Lightnings, to give a total of five, by the end of July, none arrived. The operations record book notes that the ground equipment so far supplied was inadequate to operate even one aircraft.

"My first Lightning flight was on 23 September 1960, when I flew for just under an hour", continues Jones. "The trip was supervised by Ken Goodwin, who took off in a Hunter just before me and followed me round, cutting off all the corners. On the first trip, we would take off and fly to 36,000ft, which was the standard operating height for a Lightning, then accelerate to Mach 1.3, do a few turns, turn back towards base, perform a GCA [ground-controlled approach] overshoot, go round the circuit and land off the second one. Then, the next day, I did my second trip, similar except that I went up to Mach 1.6, the idea being that, when you landed, you joined the 1,000-mile-an-hour club.

❖

"Talking with a few of the others about their first flight, they went supersonic in the climb, as they weren't used to the Lightning's steep climbing angle. But because we'd discussed it, I managed not to exceed Mach 0.98! Compared with the Hunter, the Lightning was a much bigger and heavier aeroplane. Sitting on the runway, you were much higher off the ground. When you went to taxi, you didn't have to put power on — you just released the brakes. Idle power alone was sufficient to get you to 70kt, so you taxied on the brakes all the time.

"On take-off, the enormous shove in the back was not startling, but certainly something you'd not experienced before. Things happened so rapidly. On take-off, as soon as you got airborne, you had to get the undercarriage up before you exceeded the 250kt nosewheel gear limiting speed and you'd hit 450kt to start the climb. Very rapidly that translated to 0.85, the climbing Mach number, and soon you'd be at 36,000ft. The challenge, initially, was to try and stay ahead of the aeroplane. Landing was very different from in a Hunter, even though both were swept-wing. Once you slowed down, you started to be held up by engine thrust as much as by wing lift. But it all became very easy by the end."

Through the summer of 1960, Lightnings trickled off the English Electric line at a rate of about one every two weeks and were delivered to Coltishall for No 74 Squadron. Meanwhile, Hunter flying was drastically scaled back and the engineers more than had their hands full keeping the Lightnings serviceable. In the end, every pilot on the squadron succeeded in converting to the Lightning, and there were no fatalities during the programme, a considerable achievement on so sophisticated an aircraft. By November 1960, the squadron had reached its full establishment of 12 F1s and 16 aircrew: the boss, two flight commanders and 13 pilots. That said, serviceability was low, spares proved to be in short supply and flying hours were limited, all of which slowed progress towards an operational declaration.

"Well", notes David, "they kept saying that we must be operational, but then at the same time saying, 'yes, but we want you to go to Farnborough, or to the Paris Air Show' and so on. If the war started, we'd have been operational overnight, but we were never really into quick reaction alert in a big way, because we didn't have enough serviceable aeroplanes."

In July 1960, the squadron was tasked with demonstrating four Lightnings at the SBAC show at Farnborough that September, even though, at the time, it did not actually have four aircraft. Pressure from 'on high' to mount a display stemmed partly from the RAF's desire to showcase its new aircraft, but also from the need to promote the Lightning on the export market. On 1 September, six jets positioned to Boscombe Down, from where they would operate. The team of pilots — John Howe, Jerry Cohu, Ted Nance and Alan Wright — flew their box-four routine at Farnborough to great acclaim on each day of the show, save the Tuesday when the weather precluded it. This gave members of the public their first chance to see 'the RAF's new supersonic fighter' in action. Lightning four-ships

appeared at several stations' Battle of Britain 'At Home' Days, with Mike Cooke providing a solo at certain locations.

In January 1961, snow descended onto Norfolk and No 23 Squadron's Javelins, with their 'nose-up, tail-down' ground attitude, used their jet exhausts to clear Coltishall's runway. That same month, No 74 Squadron achieved 100 flying hours on the Lightning for the first time since re-equipment.

The big press day at Coltishall for No 74 Squadron and the Lightning F1 was 22 February 1961, when the squadron had all 12 of its aircraft on the line. *The Aeroplane*'s reporters

<hr>

and photographers were there and several of their shots, scanned from glass negatives, illustrate this feature. "There was a 12-aircraft stream take-off", says David Jones, "with me as number 12 in the stream in XM147 'Papa'. We also spent time standing around and being photographed in Taylor helmets and bits of kit. The press men got very excited, standing right next to the runway. They got a welcome and a briefing from the station commander, Gp

Capt [Harold] Bird-Wilson, who had considerable presence."

When in late February 1961 a serious fire hazard was identified in the area of the ventral tank and number one engine, all aircraft had their ventral tank removed until an engineering solution could be incorporated. "Those were really good days", remarks Jones. "Without the ventral tank fitted, the F1 went like a rocket, but you didn't get a very long sortie."

Progress continued towards achieving operational status, while the aircraft, as the ORB noted, "are beginning to give slightly better serviceability". In January 1961, 74 was formally declared a 'night all-weather squadron' rather than a 'day fighter squadron'. By March it had eight pilots fully operational, and as of April all the 'original' pilots were too, leaving only the two replacement pilots to complete their training.

"We were declared operational, and we'd all flown at night by then. If push came to shove we'd have stopped playing around at airshows. But by then we were committed. It's a bit like the Red Arrows today; if war comes, they suddenly become fighter pilots. All the guys on the squadron were experienced pilots at different levels. There weren't any first-tourists; they stopped those in very early 1959, and most new people were from Cranwell."

On 16 May 1961, there was a dramatic incident involving XM141. Jim Burns was flying close-formation at high speed in a four-ship ❯

ENGLISH ELECTRIC LIGHTNING F.1

Two 14,430 lb.s.t. Rolls-Royce Avon Turbojets

Drawing by J. H. Clark, A.R.Ae.S.

© Temple Press Limited, 1961

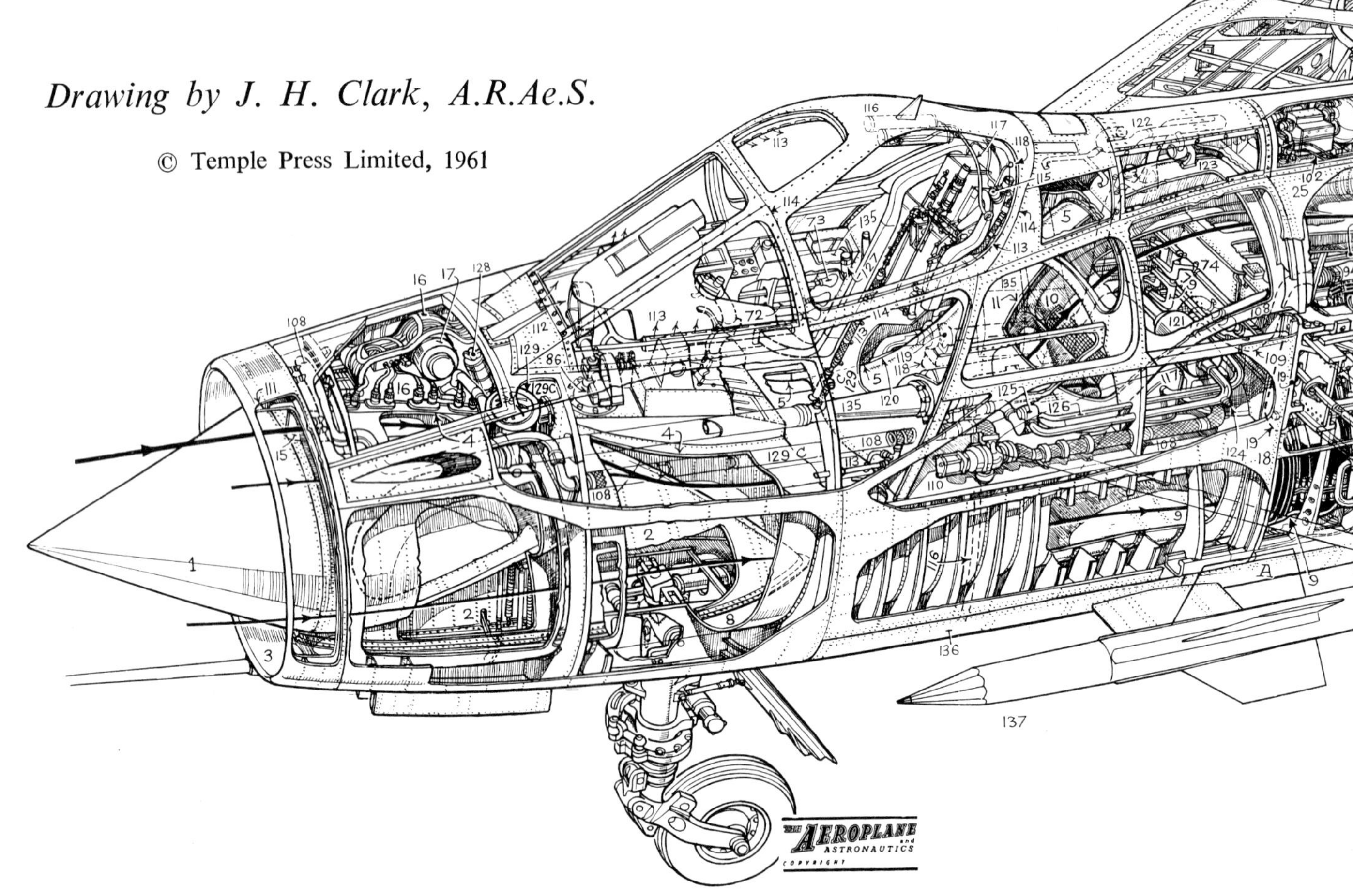

1 Nose cone: houses radar and is mounted on wheel-well box **(2)** set on floor **(8)** of engine intake **(3)**.

2 Engine air intake (top section shown at **4** down to cockpit floor, up at **5** to roof of the overwing intake **[6]** to upper engine **[7]**).

8 Floor of intake **(3)** runs straight through to lower engine **(9)**.

10 Leading edge of wing centre-section divides airflow to engines **(7 and 9)**.

11 Cut-away of top surface **(5)** to reveal bifurcation **(10)**.

12 Jet pipe of upper engine.

13 Extended jet pipe of lower engine.

14 Reheat units

15 Faired nose cone spacer providing throughway for radar electrics **(16)** into nose cone.

17 Oxygen cylinder.

18 End-frame of front fuselage (picks up to wing front fitting **[19]** of rear fuselage).

20 Rear fuselage with longeron **(20)**, strongly ribbed between-deck **(21)** and lower hoops **(22)**, engine-bay stressed top cover **(23)**,

back-end continuous frame **(24)**, stressed arch **(25)** over wing centre section with longeron plate and angle **(26)**, underwing side-panel **(27)** with similar plate longeron and angle to wing, and under-skin attachments **(28)**.

29 Rear wing spar fitting **(30)** picks up off strengthening frame **(29)**.

31 Engine main (trunnion) supports (see near **29** and longeron **[20]** near airbrakes).

32 Airbrake and double-acting hydraulic jack (electro-hydraulic selection from cockpit).

overhead Coltishall when the fin failed and the rudder separated, this the result of the aerodynamic load imposed by the adjacent aircraft. Burns landed safely, the aircraft was assessed as category 3 and repaired, but a special flying instruction was issued to define limitations until it was possible for a suitable strengthening modification to be made.

"Not only was it overhead Coltishall, but bits fell on the airfield", says Jones. "I remember seeing it happen. I was standing on the ground, watching the flypast — a box-four, straight and level, at high speed, with Jim Burns' aircraft the one in the box at the rear. It was being led by a flight commander because the boss was on the ground. He immediately leapt into his Land Rover and drove across to see how big the bits were that had fallen off."

Southern QRA was shared between units at Wattisham and Coltishall. No 74 Squadron took its turn within the constraints of its display commitments. The two alert aircraft, Q1 and Q2, were positioned on the operational readiness platform, ready to launch, while the engineers had to plan to generate further aircraft should the need arise. Holding QRA, which the squadrons did for a week at a time, was a heavy drain on resources and inevitably impacted on all other flying activity.

❖

Armament on the Lightning F1 was two fixed 30mm ADEN cannon in the nose and two Firestreak air-to-air missiles on pylons under the cockpit. English Electric brochures illustrated alternative weapon loads, with the Firestreak pack replaced by a Microcell rocket pack or by two further ADEN cannon, but these were not seen on squadron F1s, although the four-cannon fit was used at times by RAF Germany F2s and F2As. Firestreaks — which also armed No 23 Squadron's Javelins at Coltishall — were in short supply, and most photographs of No 74 Squadron Lightnings in the early days show aircraft carrying dummy Firestreaks or no missiles at all.

"In those early days on 74, we did very little QRA", Jones remembers. "The only QRA scramble I can remember doing was against one of our spy aeroplanes coming home: an incredibly high-altitude Canberra. Once I'd identified it, I was told to come home. In those days, when they scheduled those

SCANDINAVIAN SOJOURN

No 74 Squadron took eight Lightnings on a goodwill visit to Scandinavia, leaving Coltishall on 24 May 1962 and staging through Karup before arriving at Västerås, Sweden. On 26 May, they flew an eight-aircraft formation over Stockholm as part of the British Trade Fair programme, with David as number eight. Two days later, the pilots were flown to F 13 wing at Norrköping, where they made the acquaintance of the Saab J 35 Draken. This visit is remembered for the "fantastic hospitality" provided by their Swedish hosts. On 1 June, they left for Gardermoen, Norway, where they mounted a flypast over Oslo city hall, before returning home on 6 June, again via Karup.

In the squadron ORB for the month of June, Pete Botterill records, "This month marked the return to full flying by the Squadron. The shaky serviceability of a few aircraft at the beginning of the month was converted to 10 reliable aircraft by the middle of the month enabling a smooth and successful tour of Scandinavia to be achieved."

Eight Lightnings display over central Stockholm for the British Trade Fair on 26 May 1962.
ARCHIVES OF THE SWEDISH AVIATION HISTORICAL SOCIETY

flights, they didn't tell anybody or file flight plans, so they were invariably intercepted by QRA on their way back."

Preparations began for the 1961 Le Bourget Salon. Ken Goodwin, one of the RAF's most experienced display pilots — and the father of present-day Jet Pitts aerobatic performer Rich Goodwin — was to give the solo performance. On 31 May the squadron deployed its Lightnings to Creil, from where they operated for the week's duration of the Paris show.

"At Paris", says Jones, "we flew with nine aircraft, but we didn't roll nine at the show — only four. We started as a nine-ship, then the back five of us split off and the four continued and rolled. Ken Goodwin broke off for his display. He was just an outstanding pilot, the Ray Hanna of his time, an extremely nice person — and a brilliant pianist! But he was never actually on 74. We just 'borrowed' him from AFDS, who were also at Coltishall."

This was the time Jones took part 'by accident' in the final display practice on the eve of the Le Bourget show. "We had 11 aircraft at Creil and were ready for take-off to display over Le Bourget. We started up the two spares, because of the known reliability issues. I was in the second. One of the nine primary aircraft went unserviceable, so the pilot jumped

into the first spare. That then went unserviceable, but by then the time of our slot was too close, so the boss said to me, 'We've got to go. You're number nine'. I'd been involved in a lot of rehearsals, so I knew enough about it. We did some manoeuvres and at one low point the five at the back just dropped away, and the other four pulled up to do more aeros and rolls."

The inaugural NATO Tiger Meet was held at Woodbridge on 19-20 July 1961, a relatively restrained affair compared with what the event has become. There were just three Tiger Association members at that point: the Armée de l'Air's Escadron de Chasse 1/12 flying the Super Mystère B2, the US Air Force's 79th Tactical Fighter Squadron — the hosts — on the F-100D Super Sabre, and No 74 Squadron with its Lightnings.

Serious preparations then got under way for the squadron's display at Farnborough. In terms of spectacle and showmanship, this would be a step up from 1960 and would have as its highlight a nine-ship roll. In its 'Second Farnborough Show Report' issue, *The Aeroplane* printed a photo of a characteristically dramatic afterburner departure from runway 24, captioned, "No 74 Squadron's Lightnings taking off and climbing vertically before forming up for ➤

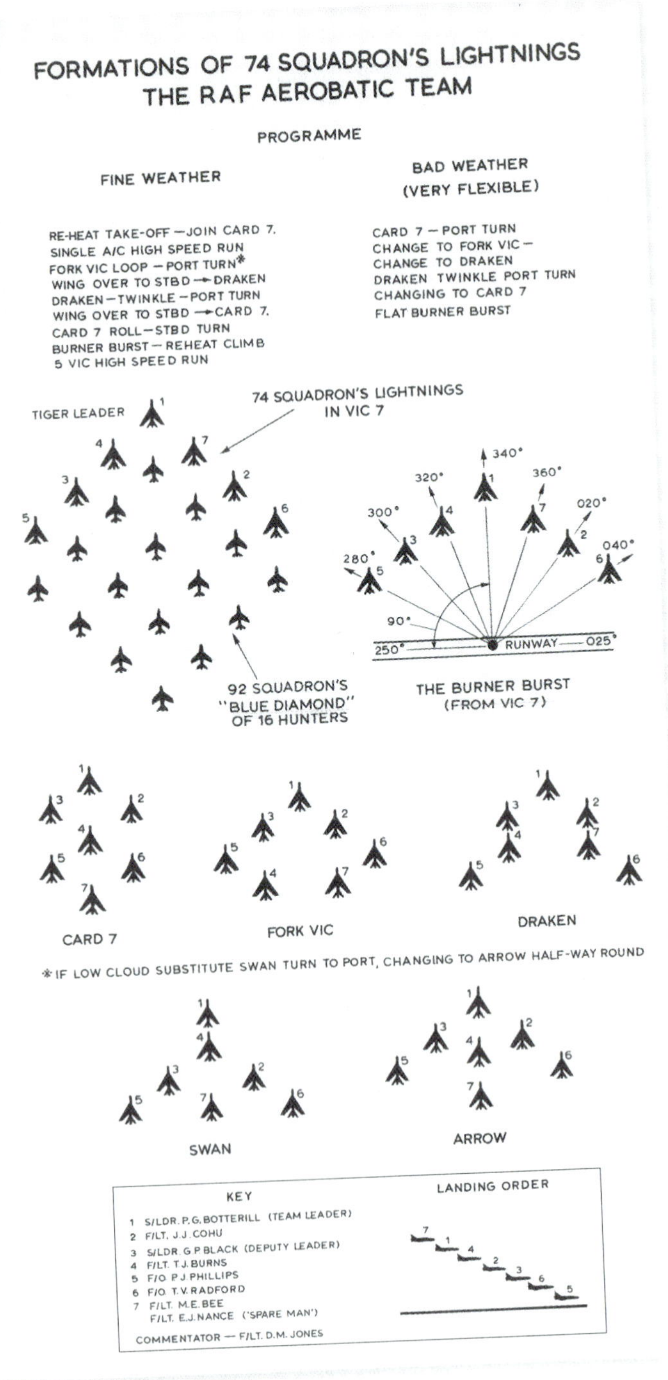

FORMATIONS OF 74 SQUADRON'S LIGHTNINGS
THE RAF AEROBATIC TEAM

PROGRAMME

FINE WEATHER

RE-HEAT TAKE-OFF — JOIN CARD 7.
SINGLE A/C HIGH SPEED RUN
FORK VIC LOOP — PORT TURN*
WING OVER TO STBD → DRAKEN
DRAKEN — TWINKLE — PORT TURN
WING OVER TO STBD → CARD 7.
CARD 7 ROLL — STBD TURN
BURNER BURST — REHEAT CLIMB
5 VIC HIGH SPEED RUN

**BAD WEATHER
(VERY FLEXIBLE)**

CARD 7 — PORT TURN
CHANGE TO FORK VIC —
CHANGE TO DRAKEN
DRAKEN TWINKLE PORT TURN
CHANGING TO CARD 7
FLAT BURNER BURST

TIGER LEADER

74 SQUADRON'S LIGHTNINGS IN VIC 7

92 SQUADRON'S "BLUE DIAMOND" OF 16 HUNTERS

THE BURNER BURST (FROM VIC 7)

CARD 7

FORK VIC

DRAKEN

* IF LOW CLOUD SUBSTITUTE SWAN TURN TO PORT, CHANGING TO ARROW HALF-WAY ROUND

SWAN

ARROW

KEY

1 S/LDR. P. G. BOTTERILL (TEAM LEADER)
2 F/LT. J. J. COHU
3 S/LDR. G. P. BLACK (DEPUTY LEADER)
4 F/LT. T. J. BURNS
5 F/O. P. J. PHILLIPS
6 F/O. T. V. RADFORD
7 F/LT. M. E. BEE
  F/LT. E. J. NANCE ('SPARE MAN')

COMMENTATOR — F/LT. D. M. JONES

LANDING ORDER

ABOVE:
The published diagram of No 74 Squadron's 1962 Farnborough routine, including the joint formation with No 92 Squadron's Hunters.

their superb nine-aircraft formation aerobatics."

"Our display slot was six or seven minutes", Jones recalls, "not a long one like the Red Arrows have these days. There was no solo Lightning from 74: just formation flying and the nine-ship roll. The solo Lightning display was by Roland Beamont or Jimmy Dell of English Electric in the T4."

John Howe was posted out with effect from 12 December 1961, three months short of the normal two years, to accept a staff job — with little opportunity for flying — at Bentley Priory. His task there was very much the build-up of the Lightning force and a rethink of Britain's air defences, this against a background of decreasing numbers of RAF fighters and a belief there could be no defence against incoming Soviet ballistic missiles. For his achievements in bringing the Lightning into RAF service, on 2 June 1962 he was awarded the Air Force Cross. As an aside, at this time RAF squadron bosses held the rank of squadron leader rather than, as now, wing commander. XM143/A, Howe's aircraft, had a squadron leader's pennant on the nose.

The unit returned to more intensive training after Farnborough, including night checks. How did it balance maintaining operational status with all the other commitments? "By definition, the squadron was fully operational. But it wasn't long before they said, 'Farnborough is coming round again'. When the bosses changed over and Pete Botterill became CO, he came in and announced, 'Right, we're now going to be a proper operational squadron. Forget all this display flying'. Despite saying this, within a few months management wanted us to go to Sweden, to Norway and to display again at Farnborough, so it all changed."

By early 1962, the squadron was achieving better serviceability and more hours from its Lightnings. "In November 1961 I got the most hours I ever flew, 19 hours 50 minutes. But it was pretty thin in some of the other months. In the whole of 1962, I got just 67 hours 30 minutes. In early 1962 we had the hydraulic modification programme, January through end-May, undertaken by an English Electric contractor's working party. That meant totally taking the aeroplanes to pieces and putting them back together. Our Lightnings were grounded, and in February and March 1962 I did no Lightning flying whatsoever. We did, though, go two at a time to No 229 OCU at Chivenor for a week, just to get some Hunter flying."

No 74 Squadron's Lightnings started to become available again in March, April and May 1962. Not having flown the type for some long time, pilots had to undergo three sorties in the simulator and a dual check ride in the Hunter T7 before resuming operations.

On 26 April, Fighter Command announced that 74 was to provide the official RAF aerobatic team for 1962, following on from No 92 Squadron's Blue Diamonds with its Hunters. Good news, but with a serious impact on squadron efficiency? "Disastrous from the operational point of view, because it meant that we had to have nine aircraft available at all times."

The fins and spines of 74's Lightnings were painted black at Coltishall that August, with the tiger's head superimposed on a white circle and the code letter now in yellow on the fin. The ORB records, "With glistening aircraft resplendant [sic] with their black fins, the Squadron looks forward eagerly to the culmination of the year's efforts at the SBAC Show."

Farnborough in September 1962 was to be the highlight of the season. It was decided to mount a combined, co-ordinated display between Nos 74 and 92 Squadrons. This meant Pete Botterill and Brian Mercer, OC No 92 Squadron, had to work together — and 92 was far more experienced in formation aerobatics. The routine started with an initial formation of 23 aeroplanes: seven Lightnings, which took off first, and 16 Hunters. With two squadron bosses, who led the formation?

"It was Pete Botterill", says Jones, "because the Lightnings were at the front of this great 23-aircraft formation that did a few gentle manoeuvres before it split. From then on it was co-ordinated, with Brian Mercer calling the shots and the timings. 74 would come on with seven Lightnings, then 92 with 16 Hunters. Eventually, 74 would quit and 92 would do some of its more sophisticated stuff. I was the official commentator for that, alternating day-in, day-out with John Vickery, the No 92 Squadron commentator. On one of my off-days, I flew with Brian Mercer in the display, in the Hunter T7. You wouldn't do it these days, would you? It was spectacular. Very, very impressive. All parts of it went well, and it was quite a long display. The public certainly got their money's worth."

> ## *The aerobatic team was disastrous from an operational point of view*

On 3 August, the squadron had finally taken delivery of a two-seat Lightning, T4 XM974/T, which it took to Farnborough. "Even so, my first flight in the T4 was not until 18 October. Its arrival meant that George Black, the QFI [qualified flying instructor], could give us a proper dual check and we were finally doing instrument ratings in a representative aircraft. But in my entire time on No 74 Squadron, I did a total of six hours in the T4."

74 returned to something approaching normal operations after Farnborough, including QRA. The weather in early 1963 severely impacted activity, but nevertheless David still managed some Lightning trips. Examination of his logbook underlines the fact that the F1 was short on fuel tankage and was incapable of in-flight refuelling. As a result, very few sorties exceeded one hour. "Despite the hard winter, I got a reasonable amount of flying: 15 hours 15 minutes, F1 and T4, in January and 10 hours 20 minutes, F1 and T4, in February. Not bad."

❖

During his time on the squadron, David featured — albeit without being named — in an RAF pilot recruiting advertisement that appeared in newspapers and magazines on a near-daily basis over a period of several months. He came to be selected for the photo completely by chance. "Somebody from MoD [the Ministry of Defence] came to Coltishall and I was told, 'Dave, you're not flying until this afternoon. Go and get your kit on,

see what he wants.' So, I went and stood by an aeroplane, and the chap kept telling me to look this way or that."

He also appeared, yet more anonymously, in *Streaked Lightning*. Two Lightnings coded 'A' featured in the film; one was the 'real' XM143/A while the identity of the second — the imposter — is unknown. David flew two sorties on 19 June 1962 for the cameras. The air-to-air sequences were filmed from the side door of a Hastings or the rear seat of a Meteor T7. He also featured as 'the pilot' in his cockpit (actually the simulator) and recorded the pilot end of the RT conversation between 'Lightning 74' and the control tower,

although he describes the scripted content as "a bit iffy."

David's time on the squadron came to an end in the spring of 1963, after almost five years. His last flight with 74 was on 8 April and his posting date a week later. New units were forming on the Lightning F2 and, with his experience and 217 Lightning hours under his belt, he joined No 19 Squadron at Leconfield. How does he look back on those early days of the Lightning F1? "I realise how lucky I was to be part of those exciting times", he reflects, "and will never forget how hard the engineers on No 74 Squadron had to work to make it all possible." **A**

A spectacular display-closing 'burner burst' by 74's Lightnings at Farnborough on 8 September 1962 — no qualms about crowd overflights here. R. L. WARD

VIKING'S SECOND COMING

A classic British airliner is coming back together at Blackbushe Airport, and with exciting plans surrounding its future

WORDS AND PHOTOGRAPHY:
BEN DUNNELL

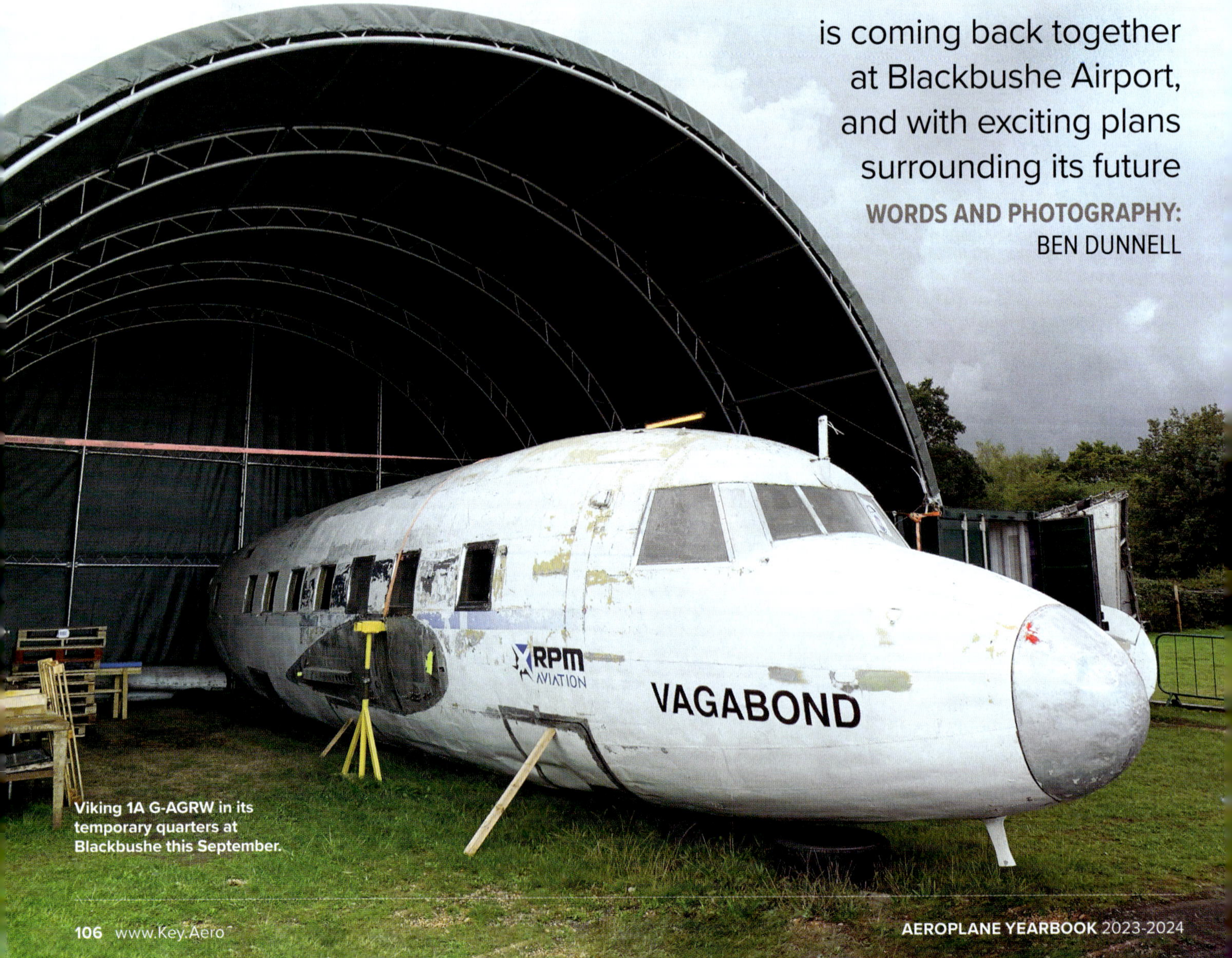

Viking 1A G-AGRW in its temporary quarters at Blackbushe this September.

Everyone could have been forgiven a moment of jubilation. As Vickers Viking 1A G-AGRW rolled through the gates of Blackbushe Airport on 2 May this year, it represented the culmination of many fervently held ambitions. But the volunteer team from the Blackbushe Heritage Trust knew it was also the point at which the real work started.

A few months down the line, and what a splendid spectacle is on view at the Hampshire airfield. The 1946-vintage airliner is partially under cover, a rare luxury, and its transformation into a museum-piece is well under way. What's more, it's all happened in surprisingly quick time, because it needed to. It was in March last year that word reached Peter Brown, now chairman of the trustees, of the Viking's plight. Sitting outside at Bad Vöslau Airport in Austria, it had to be moved or else it would not survive. A previous idea of bringing G-AGRW back to Britain for use in a Wellington reconstruction project had fallen through. The prospect of its being scrapped, says Peter, "was something we couldn't accept". The charitable trust was formed, support sought, and a plan put in place.

As Peter Brown comments, "The Viking and the airport are fundamentally part of each other". Nine airlines equipped with the Bristol Hercules-powered twin were based there until 1960, when Blackbushe Airport in its original form — often described as 'London's second airport' — was closed by the government. With the development of Gatwick, those carriers which used Blackbushe were 'encouraged' to move there. It was thanks to the tenacity of AVM Don Bennett, of wartime Pathfinder Force fame, that the aerodrome reopened in truncated form for general aviation use during 1962. Peter, incidentally, worked for Bennett as his operations manager. Today the area around the control tower is the only part of the old pre-1960 airport that's still in use, and this is central to the trust's objectives.

Expansion proposals on the part of the airport's current owners will, if approved, transform the scene. They hope to build a new terminal, hangars, clubhouse and associated buildings in the southern part of the site, which would replace a variety of temporary structures, and allow the current tower and terminal to become a heritage centre. It has been a complex process, not least because the airport sits on common land. But the vision is ready to be put into practice, and it involves the Viking, when restored, sitting on the tarmac outside.

It was a close-run thing as to whether G-AGRW, otherwise known as *Vagabond* — its name with British European Airways — would be salvageable at all. While it had passed into the ownership of the Austrian Aviation Museum at Bad Vöslau, south-west of Vienna, the Viking was not relevant to its collection. "The aircraft was falling apart", says trust secretary Dave Payne, who had earlier sought to recover G-AGRW himself. "It

was becoming a hazard for the airport. They couldn't manage it."

When the Blackbushe Heritage Trust was set up, assistance came in from many quarters. Pat Marchant of Oxford Airport-based RPM Aviation was enlisted thanks to his expertise in aircraft dismantling and transportation. He and another trustee, ex-Eagle Aviation apprentice Phil Johns, were key figures in organising the road move from Austria. Among various financial contributions, a generous donation was received from British Airways' Better World Community Fund, in keeping with the project's aims to be a community and educational attraction.

Pat and colleagues dismantled the aeroplane between 21 and 27 April, a process that involved stripping out the decidedly unoriginal interior features from its days at the Schwechat McDonald's. "The flooring", he says, "was chipboard about an inch-and-a-half thick. It was very much reinforced. There were angle iron supports with a huge air conditioning unit in them, and if you look in one of the engine bays on the aircraft you can see there's an air-con unit in that still that needs removal and disposal. All the ducting down the cabin was removed on site. The plan was to remove all of the floor, but time was against us and it didn't go as easily as we'd hoped. We did take out the wall linings and the loft insulation behind them."

Apart from being necessary for the future restoration, this was all a useful weight-saving exercise prior to the journey from Bad Vöslau to Blackbushe. Having negotiated a rather tricky roundabout at the entrance to the Austrian airfield, it proved quite a straightforward undertaking. However, as Blackbushe Airport managing director Chris Gazzard adds, "It sat in a lay-by in Dover for a few days, waiting for a follow-me vehicle. This was because of its length. As it was a bank holiday weekend, it could only come on Tuesday morning, so the driver had to sleep in his cab…"

Both Chris and the airport's business development

The interior awaits fitting-out, but a lot of the additions made for the aircraft's use by a McDonald's restaurant in Austria, such as installation of an air conditioning system and a heavy chipboard floor, have gone.

manager have become trustees. Practical support has come in the form of the temporary hangar, offering that all-important element of shelter as restoration takes place, and two neighbouring containers, one a bookshop and storage area, the other a workshop for smaller items. "We wouldn't have been able to do it without the backing of the airport", says Dave Payne. And the same goes for the myriad other supporters, whether through provision of funding, expertise or other help in kind, who are all acknowledged on the banners displayed in front of the hangar.

Inside, *Vagabond* is making the transition into a proper museum exhibit for the first time in its life. The wings are stored pending refurbishment, while the fuselage receives attention. Scaffolding will be erected around it, up to the height of the windows, and the roof area thoroughly inspected for leaks and any damage. Repairs will then be performed as necessary. After that, the next step is due to see the fuselage stripped down, and the top of it painted white while the scaffolding is still up. Only then will it be raised further off the ground onto trestles, so as to permit inspection of the main belly area, and reinstallation of the main spar. If all goes to plan, next spring could see G-AGRW back on its wheels.

The group wants to deal with the belly before tackling the floor, since access to the baggage compartments will probably be necessary. Some of the baggage doors have been damaged and need repair. When the floor goes in, it will most likely be honeycomb flooring from a more modern airliner that's been scrapped, this being a lightweight, dependable and durable solution given the need for public access. In that context, discussions are under way as to how best make the aeroplane wheelchair-accessible. Quite a lot of the windows need to be replaced as they had McDonald's stickers applied to them in the aircraft's previous life.

The search is on for pairs of seats ready to go straight into the aircraft. This means the seating will not be faithful to the Viking's original BEA fit, but practical considerations come first. An excellent upholsterer is already a member of the team, and he will be responsible for finishing the interior as a period BEA Admiral-class machine, with red carpeting up to the windows and a beige roof. As for the external livery, the decision has been made to adopt an Eagle Airways scheme on one side, given the carrier's strong Blackbushe connection, and — pending approval from British Airways — BEA colours on the other. Eagle retained the basic Admiral-class livery, so this is a good combination.

The trust is looking to involve apprentices in the restoration, not least from Farnborough Airport and Gulfstream. It gives them hands-on experience with an aeroplane, and contributes to meeting the project's educational objectives. As things stand, the regular, core workforce is about half-a-dozen strong, and new additions with suitable skills are always welcome.

> **"** *The focus will always be on types with a Blackbushe connection* **"**

Putting a schedule on realising the trust's museum ambitions is difficult, dependent as it is on the airport's redevelopment programme getting the go-ahead. It is certainly not beyond the bounds of possibility that other aircraft will be added, and the airport, says Chris Gazzard, would be "very happy" to welcome them. The focus remains on G-AGRW at the moment, and will always be placed on types with a proper Blackbushe connection. There are plenty of those, so rich is its history as both a military and a civilian airfield. Given time, this will hopefully be remembered in the most appropriate way possible. **Ⓐ**

For more information and to support the project, visit www.blackbusheheritagetrust.com

One of the Bristol Hercules engines, complete with propeller, its nacelle and the tailcone receive attention.

Provision of undercover accommodation was a major boost. About half-a-dozen volunteers work regularly on the project, both on weekdays and weekends, with many others having signed up.

Today's Blackbushe Airport is a very busy general aviation airfield, with about 100 resident aircraft and multiple based flying schools. The Viking helps recall the site's pre-1960 past as home to 'London's second airport'.

A VAGABOND'S EXISTENCE

Constructed as a Viking 1A, G-AGRW (c/n 115) originally went to the Ministry of Supply before going to British European Airways during September 1946, bearing the name *Vagabond*. It was subsequently operated by Autair and Hunting-Clan, the latter of which was based at Blackbushe, prior to being retired in early 1968. The aircraft's final flight was to Soesterberg air base in the Netherlands on 15 February that year. There it was grounded, going on to become one of a trio of Vikings converted into the nearby Avio Resto restaurant.

Upon the death of the proprietor, G-AGRW went via Germany to Austria, being displayed on the Vienna Airport viewing deck until 1999. Then it was moved the short distance to a McDonald's restaurant in Schwechat, painted in spurious Austrian Airlines colours — thanks to the national carrier's sponsorship of its refurbishment — and mounted on three plinths, being used to host children's parties. Paper cups, candles, crayons and the like were found under the floor on its recent recovery. Deemed surplus to requirements, the Viking passed to the Austrian Aviation Museum at Bad Vöslau in 2011, and there it stayed until acquisition by the Blackbushe Heritage Trust last year. One other example is preserved in the UK: G-AGRU at the Brooklands Museum, which was also part of the Soesterberg restaurant.

"Honourable men seeking redress"

The US troop carrier aircrew of D-Day: poorly trained, cowardly or just low-grade? It's time to debunk these myths **WORDS:** ADAM BERRY

C-47A 42-92717 *Stoy Hora* led the 440th TCG's elements of the D-Day operation, in the hands of group commander Col Frank Krebs. On board were 16 men from the 506th Parachute Infantry Regiment, as well as a war correspondent. USAF

On the morning of 6 June 1944, 14 troop carrier groups belonging to IX Troop Carrier Command of the US Ninth Air Force entered the skies over Normandy, carrying the parachute and initial glider elements of two American airborne divisions. These were the men flying the Douglas C-47 Skytrains and troop-carrying gliders, taking thousands of battle-ready soldiers to their drop or landing zones.

By daylight on D-Day, hundreds found themselves far from their correct drop zones, often fighting alongside unfamiliar units. Of course, many lay dead in the fields and marshlands surrounding towns like Sainte-Mère-Église and Carentan. Almost from the very moment their boots touched French soil, there was scrutiny of the performance of IX TCC's aircrew, many of whom were labelled as cowboy pilots, ill-trained, inexperienced and even cowardly. But has our perception of what happened that fateful morning been warped by the poor research of those entrusted to tell the stories of that day? Did the very earliest D-Day historians fail to look at both sides of the coin?

It started in a literary sense with S. L. A. Marshall's 1962 book *Night Drop: The American Airborne Invasion of Normandy*. Looking at Marshall's references, it soon becomes apparent that at no stage of his research did he confer with any troop carrier aircrew. Just 17 years from the conclusion of World War Two, he had an opportunity to interview hundreds of those who crewed the C-47s that night, yet he chose not to. Much of his data is drawn from after-action reports and interviews with survivors of the Normandy campaign from the two airborne divisions. That same information was compiled by the 14 troop carrier groups which flew the missions to Normandy on 6-7 June. Had Marshall consulted these, his assertions may well have differed.

The American author Stephen Ambrose, who released no fewer than four best-sellers, had this to say on page 198 of his *D-Day*: "The pilots were afraid. For most of the pilots of Troop Carrier Command, this was their first combat mission. They had not been trained for night flying, or for flak or bad weather. Their C-47s were designed to carry cargo and passengers. They were neither armed nor armored. Their gas tanks were neither protected nor self-sealing. The possibility of mid-air collision was on every pilot's mind…"

This can be viewed as a suggestion of cowardice, of distrust in the machines they flew and, most

> ## *Many of IX TCC's aircrew were labelled as cowboy pilots*

importantly, of an overall lack of adequate training. As with Marshall, Ambrose relied on the testimony of many former US paratroopers, but not troop carrier aircrew. How could he have known they were all afraid, or concerned about collisions?

In 2002, the late Randy Hils, whose father had served in the 440th Troop Carrier Group, published an article. Randy was concerned by how troop carrier aircrew were being perceived, so he began to tackle the issue head-on. Throughout the nineties several veterans sent letters to Stephen Ambrose, addressing his comments and asking him to consider changes. His typical responses were that he could not make amendments due to contractual reasons, or there was simply no reply at all. This culminated, in September 2001, with a face-to-face encounter between Ambrose, troop carrier veteran Michael Ingrisano and his wife, Nancy. In the short time Nancy had with Ambrose, she compelled him to review the documentation and to have errata sheets included with all subsequent copies of his book that were sold. At that stage, Ambrose "promised to make it up" and

ABOVE:
A mass paratroop training exercise prior to the Normandy landings.
NATIONAL ARCHIVES AND RECORDS ADMINISTRATION

ABOVE:
Maj Gen Matthew Ridgway, who commanded the 82nd Airborne Division through Sicily, Italy, and Normandy, recognised early on how important joint air-ground training was. US ARMY

instructed Michael and Nancy to send him letters he would follow up on. They went unanswered. His son Hugh would later claim that the attacks on his father were not a discussion but a diatribe.

British writer Max Hastings was challenged in January 1986 over his opinions on troop carrier pilots and aircrew by Col William Parkhill, a pilot and former executive officer of the 441st Troop Carrier Group. Hastings admitted in his response that he was "unfamiliar" with the points raised by Parkhill and agreed "the whole issue needed further consideration". Several other publications relating to the airborne missions over Normandy — or the battle for Normandy as a whole — appear to have regurgitated much of this information.

One degrading accusation aimed at troop carrier pilots is that they were the dregs of the US Army Air Corps' aviation cadet programmes. There is simply no evidence to suggest this. Those who ended up flying with troop carrier units graduated from classes with men who became fighter and bomber pilots. Many didn't even see active 'front-line' duty. To cite just one example, Flying Cadet Edison Heins graduated from the Air Corps Advanced Flying School at Kelly Field, Texas, on 11 July 1941, as a fighter pilot in the same class as 'Doolittle Raider' Richard Cole. He later requested a transfer to C-47s and, as a captain, became the personal pilot of Maj Gen Paul L. Williams, the commander of IX TCC.

They weren't selected to fly transports because they were poor pilots. Many had demonstrated special abilities or may have lacked the requirements to become a fighter pilot. It was necessary to meet the height and weight criteria in order to fly fighters. For instance, in the aviation cadet programme, anyone taller than 6ft 9in and heavier than 160lb could not train to be a fighter pilot and was instead pushed into other roles. Physical attributes like strength were also assessed when choosing where to post a cadet, as pilots of four-engined heavy bombers had to demonstrate greater strength over longer periods than a fighter pilot needed. A bomber pilot had to physically manhandle his aircraft to and from a target for, in rare cases, more than 15 hours and often with damage.

And, quite apart from anything else, it was necessary to direct pilots towards the parts of the AAF where they were most needed. In May 1943, when the initial plans for D-Day were first discussed, it became apparent that a greater troop carrier force would be required. At that stage, just two wings and seven TCGs existed in Europe. More would be needed for the delivery of multiple airborne divisions across a broad front. As part of the build-up of forces, any pilots pushed towards twin-engine pilot training in the aviation cadet programme were often assigned to fledgling TCGs. As many as 40 per cent of those who ended up as glider pilots within the TCGs with a service pilot rating had been drafted on account of their pre-war flying experience.

"...nearly all of my class at flying school were ordered to troop carrier [units], and the following class was worse. They had all been trained as fighter pilots!"
Lt Col Dwight C. Baier, pilot, 438th Troop Carrier Group

Many were selected to fly transports thanks to their pre-war experiences, too. Group commanders like Col James J. Roberts, a pre-war airline pilot with more than 10,000 hours flying the DC-2 and DC-3, were led to postings based on their knowledge of the aircraft. Col Maurice Beach, CO of the 53rd Troop Carrier Wing, flew twin-engined aircraft with the air corps. Other group commanders such as Clayton Stiles and Hamish McLelland, as well as squadron bosses, boasted hours of flying time on aircraft they would go on to captain in World War Two.

RIGHT:
Turf and Sport Special was the name applied to C-47A 42-92841, operated by the 61st TCS, 314th TCG at Saltby. This Skytrain is preserved by the Air Mobility Command Museum at Dover AFB, Delaware. USAF

Of the 14 TCGs that operated on D-Day, only four had dropped paratroopers during a combat mission. Those were the 61st, 313th, 314th and 316th, each of which disgorged elements of the 82nd Airborne Division over Sicily and Italy in 1943. One of the primary criticisms members of these groups had in preparing for the Sicilian and Italian missions was a lack of training time in co-operation with the airborne divisions. These units were rushed in from the States, having carried out a small number of unrealistic mock exercises. Once in theatre, practice drops were virtually non-existent. Soon these aircraft were in the skies over Sicily, being shot to hell by their own navy, following which the AAF finally accepted that increased emphasis should be placed on training.

After the Sicilian debacle, in which the 82nd Airborne Division was left widely scattered across the battlefield, its commander, Maj Gen Matthew Ridgway, argued his division should be allowed to train directly with the troop carrier units that had deployed it during Operation 'Husky', as the division's report goes on to explain: "Profiting from the lessons learned in Sicily, he repeatedly and vigorously urged a minimum of three weeks combined Air-Ground training with the Troop Carrier Command. He urgently

recommended that the 82nd be immediately concentrated in the Kairouan area for the purpose of re-organization, re-equipping, and training."

As of 29 July 1943, Ridgway had been aware of the army's intention to use his division in the invasion of Italy, and therefore wanted both it and Troop Carrier Command to be better-prepared. Regardless of the perceived importance of his division's involvement in the mission

> ## 66 *There is no evidence the pilots were the dregs of the cadets* 99

to come, which was changed to accommodate them, the army was slow in withdrawing the 82nd and re-equipping it for the combat that lay ahead. Just 19 days before the date of the mission, only half of Ridgway's division had been withdrawn from Sicily. As the report goes on to say, "Gone was the expectation of any substantial air-ground training with Troop Carrier Command. It was too late. Every effort had to be concentrated on getting the troops

back from Sicily and re-equipping them."

When the 52nd TCW arrived in England, it was joined by a fifth group, the 315th, which had not dropped paratroopers in anger to date. Nine more groups across two further wings were despatched to the UK to bring IX TCC to full strength. A lack of experience can be cited, but this is inevitable and could not be avoided on D-Day as experienced troop carrier pilots were rare. However, that cannot be presented as a reasonable argument for the mis-drops because there is such variance in the performances of the groups across those with and without experience. Perhaps the most catastrophic and costly mis-drop on D-Day involved elements of the HQ Company, 3rd Battalion, 507th Parachute Infantry Regiment, seven aircraft-loads of men, around the village of Graignes. They were dropped by elements of the 61st TCG, which had deployed paratroopers into combat at least twice before. Yet one of the best drops was into DZ 'D' by the 441st TCG, a group with no prior experience.

Perhaps the most impressive drop that night was by the 315th TCG. Remember, this was a group that prior to D-Day had never dropped paratroopers in combat, and which just one month earlier had been ➔

 USAF

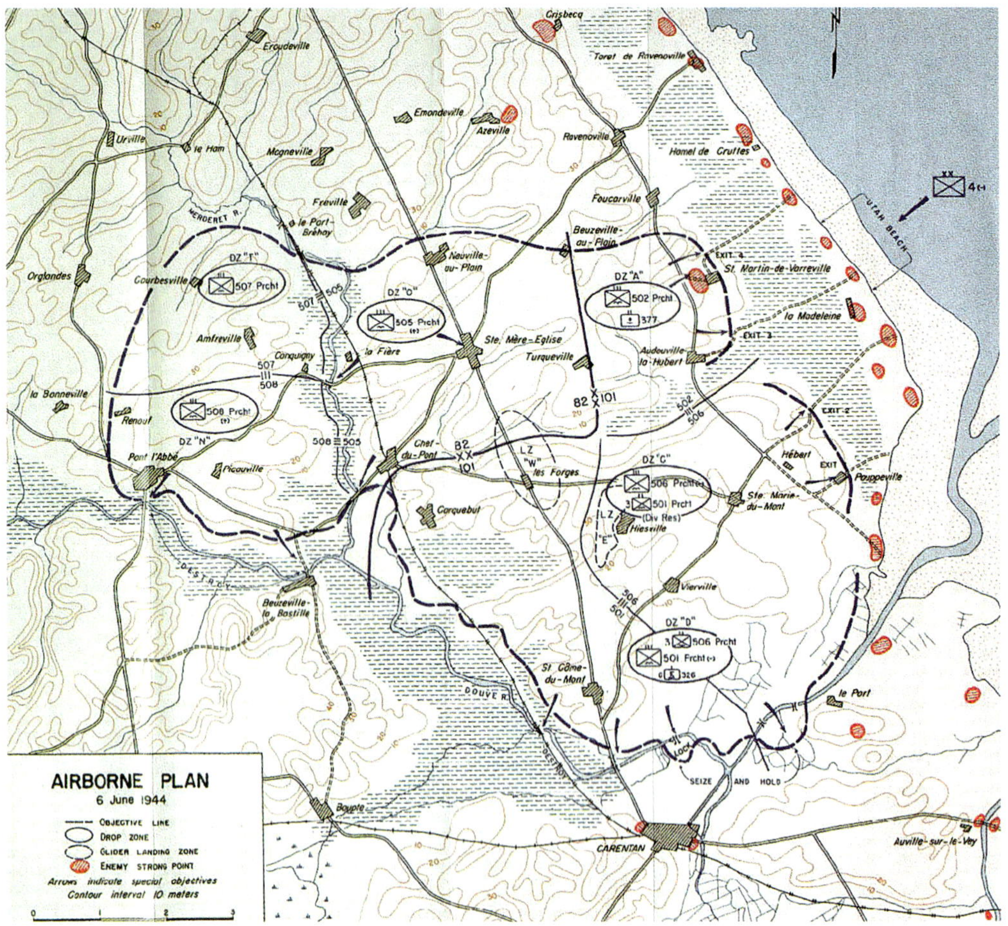

ABOVE AND OPPOSITE: Period US Army maps showing (above) the overall plan for the D-Day airborne assault, and the actual drop patterns achieved by the 82nd and 101st Airborne Divisions, which illustrate the degree of scatter.

US ARMY

under-strength, with only two squadrons, a smaller complement of aircraft and fewer pilots. It had spent its war to date flying search and rescue missions or delivering supplies. The 310th and 309th TCSs were formed at the end of April and the beginning of May respectively, and although seasoned pilots were brought in from other groups, these two squadrons were 'green'. This group and its four squadrons dropped the 1st Battalion, 505th PIR, 82nd Airborne Division, which reported an excellent drop.

Was this achieved despite a lack of training? Were they just lucky? It happened as a result of performing formation training flights, with or without paratroopers on board, as often as the English weather allowed.

The suggestion the TCGs had not trained in the run-up to the invasion is not true, and it is ridiculous to even suggest so. Between 15 March and 27 May 1944, IX Troop Carrier Command executed no fewer than

> ## 66 *It is ridiculous to even suggest that the groups had not trained* 99

33 combined troop carrier/airborne exercises in the UK, in co-operation with the 82nd and 101st Airborne Divisions, the British 1st and 6th Airborne Divisions, and the Polish 1st Independent Parachute Brigade. Though their success varied, there are suggestions that one of the primary reasons for this was the liaison between the airborne units and the troop carrier group that would deploy them.

That March, the 316th TCG at Cottesmore had noted a greater level of success in deploying British airborne forces than American. This is what it had to say: "Close liaison supplied by the British 1st Airborne Division was an important contributing factor. In the field of paratroop work, we have much to learn from the British in the way of liaison. Any Airborne unit which is expected to furnish troops in practice or actual drops should supply an Officer, whose sole duty is to work out all the details with our operations and S-2 staffs over a

period of weeks rather than days. By working together in this manner the success of a mission is virtually assured, assuming the weather is favourable and there is no failure of equipment."

These training exercises include only those organised at command and wing levels. All groups were supported in the execution of such taskings as regularly as the weather permitted. In the case of the 315th TCG, its early experiences in flying group formations with no cargo showed just how difficult this could be at low level. On several formations in poor drop conditions it found the aircraft were bouncing from one altitude to another, and pilots were seldom able to maintain flight on the wing of another aeroplane. This took an immense amount of practice, and to achieve acceptable levels the group flew multiple formations each day, including night-time flights.

"'Untrained?' I certainly didn't feel untrained. I had 18 months of technical and academic training, which included 400 hours' pilot time before I joined the 316th Troop Carrier Group in Sicily in late 1943. By D-Day I had acquired over 800 hours of total flight time. Some of this involved miscellaneous supply missions, but was primarily devoted to close day-night formation flying, practice drops of paratroops, glider pulls, short-field landings, instrument flight training, etc. We all knew the invasion of Europe was coming and we concentrated on perfecting our skills on a daily basis. Pilots were rigorously trained and routinely tested to maintain their eligibility for a green card instrument rating — which was required of all first pilots"
1st Lt Julian Rice, 316th Troop Carrier Group

On the formation of the 309th TCS, Maj Smylie Stark gathered all his pilots together in the base theatre at Spanhoe and spoke to them about the job that lay ahead. He emphasised how they were expected to be among the very best, and training would be intense. His squadron alone flew formation practice on 17 of the 31 days in May, including twice in one day. Three of those flights involved dropping paratroopers with successful or good results. The remaining days of the month were used for classroom sessions.

1st Lt Donald Orcutt, flight leader, 440th Troop Carrier Group

A starting point for assessing the mis-drops would be to consider the typical US paratrooper load. It is commonly accepted that the paratroopers entered combat with loads far exceeding what they would typically carry. We could look in some detail at how this is possible, but it is relevant because it affects the aircraft's stall speed, forcing it to fly beyond the typical jump speed for a drop. The weight of the paratroopers only contributes to a tremendous opening shock and the loss of equipment.

A typical manifest shows the 17 paratroopers of E Company, 508th PIR, 82nd Airborne Division, who jumped from C-47 42-92841 of the 61st Troop Carrier Squadron, 314th Troop Carrier Group, flying from Saltby in Lincolnshire. Firstly, the aircraft was carrying 1,141lb of equipment in four A-5 drop containers slung below the fuselage in 'para-racks'. The 17 paratroopers, assuming the average weight was around 160-170lb — 1st Lt Richard Winters of E/506th weighed 165 — completely un-equipped would equate to around 3,060lb. In addition, the aircraft was crewed by six men on D-Day, making another 1,080lb, bringing the C-47 close to its 6,000lb lift capacity.

Additional weight for each paratrooper would, virtually as standard, be close to 80lb, adding a further 1,300lb to the gross weight. Again, this harmed the aircrew's ability to drop the paratroopers at the required speed. Coupling this problem with how the paratroopers were jumped on practice missions, often without proper combat loads and without bundles under the aircraft, meant the aircrew were not gaining experience in dropping a heavier-than-standard load and how doing so affected aircraft performance.

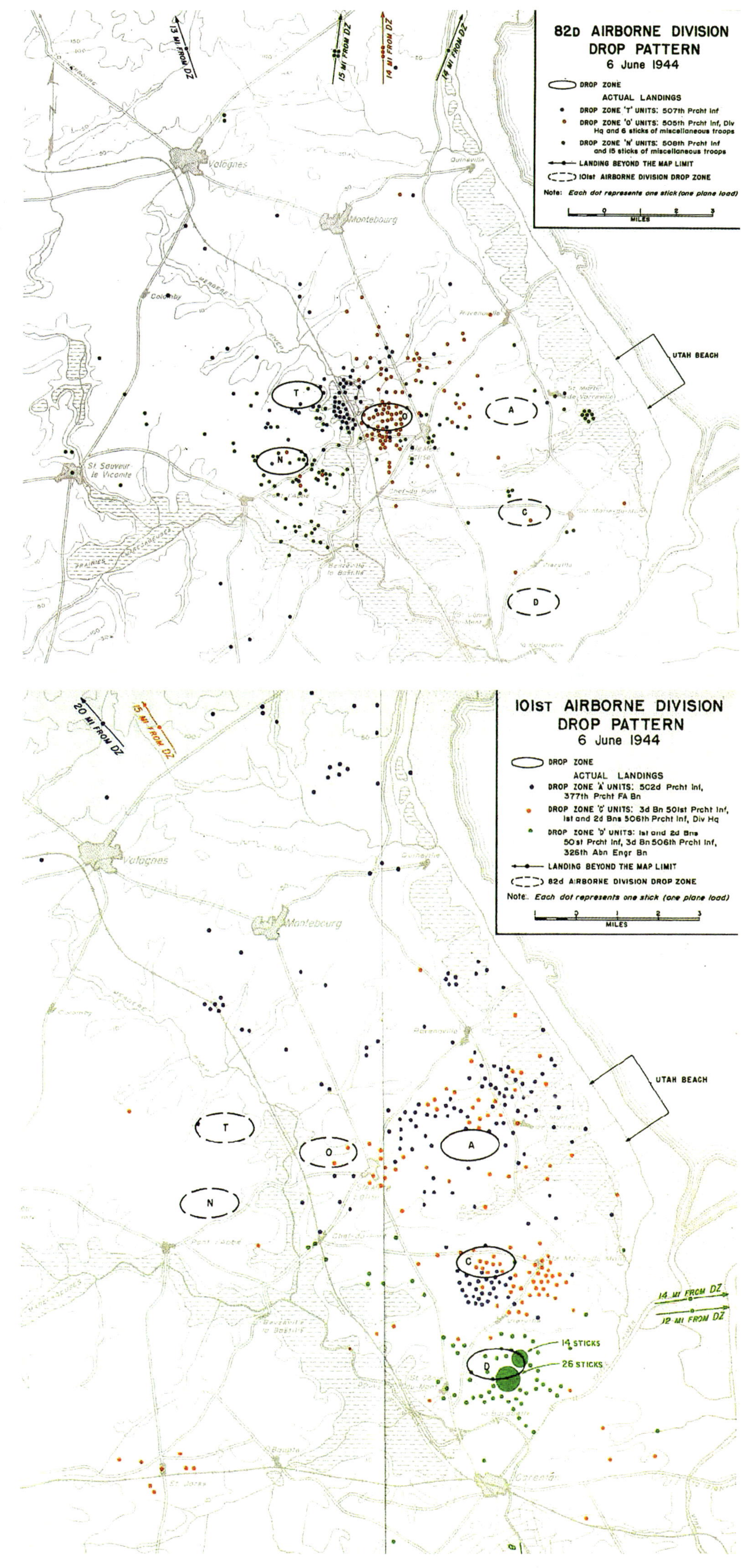

The most significant factor on D-Day was the cloud bank. The 21st Weather Squadron was assigned to IX TCC with detachments of six or seven men typically led by one officer assigned to each airfield or HQ site. Like flying control, as air traffic control was known, each section provided weather updates locally but would obtain its information from a more central command. If a group was operating solely by itself on a formation flight, the weather information was obtained and analysed by the detachment assigned to that group. For an exercise planned by the wing, details of the weather would come from wing HQ. Additional information was added by a group if more localised conditions affected it. On D-Day, the weather forecasting was provided by IX TCC, being passed down through each wing and to the groups. It would have come directly from the same reports by met stations that other units of both the AAF and RAF relied on that day. IX TCC was particularly interested in the weather from the embarkation points, along the flight routes, and at each initial point (turning point), but most critically at the drop zones.

At no stage during the briefing of the groups were they informed that a cloud bank would be covering the western coastline of the Cotentin peninsula and for some miles inland. Had they known, they could have adjusted the flight paths and altitudes flown between the final initial points running up to the DZ. When the groups hit the western coast, they were met by a dense cloud bank reported as being as low as 500ft, rising to a height of 2,500ft and some miles in depth.

Like their bomber counterparts, troop carrier crews were trained to 'fan out' a formation to limit the risk of collisions in poor conditions. This was achieved by aircraft ascending, descending, or turning to port or starboard, leading to them flying at different altitudes with greater separation than was typical for a regular formation. It did reduce the risk of collision, but had to be immensely precise to maintain a formation. This was because the formation lights on each aircraft were designed to be seen only when viewed from precisely the correct angle, which could not be done with a 'fanned-out' formation. Each aircraft would have struggled to know where the others were, whether deep in the cloud or not. To counter this, some squadrons opted to fly above the clouds, in formation, but at around 2,500-3,000ft.

"When we turned to cross over Jersey and Guernsey, we saw they were almost completely obscured by the low cloud deck. We were in our proper position, following closely behind and slightly above the flight ahead. Without warning, the flight in front of us dimmed their formation lights, and as we dropped into the clouds, I lost sight of them completely. My wingmen were tucked in tightly as they should be and I turned my formation lights to bright so they could keep me in sight. At that moment, as far as I know, I was leading the rest of the invasion airborne assault!"
1st Lt Louis R. Emerson Jr, 437th Troop Carrier Group

*"Suddenly, without warning, the s*** hit the fan! Just as we started to cross the beach area, we flew into a 1,500ft-high wall of heavy land fog that blanketed our entire portion of the formation. Not only did the critical blue lights vanish from sight, but [all the airplanes] in the formation disappeared. It was impossible for me to see my own wing. Now the fear of enemy fire was secondary. The immediate concern was mid-air collisions from the planes all around. In the darkness of the cockpit, the [...] air speed, altimeter and artificial horizon instruments demanded immediate attention"*
1st Lt Julian Rice, 316th Troop Carrier Group

Aircrew were left with a quick decision to make. Should they continue flying through thick clouds with no indication of whether the aircraft in their formation were still nearby, or fly above or below the clouds with little idea of when they

would end? It appears the cloud bank did break up before the drop zones were reached, but for each scenario, this presented a problem.

"As we neared the drop zone, I was faced with an important decision! Was it better to drop down and fly through the clouds and risk having the formation break up with the possibility of mid-air collisions or to stay above and drop the paratroopers at an altitude that would cause them to become widely separated?"
Maj Benjamin F. Kendig, commanding officer, 44th Troop Carrier Squadron, 316th Troop Carrier Group

Scenario one meant a formation was leaving the clouds at roughly the right height but with no discernible formation remaining. Therefore, pilots were scanning the skies, their aircraft often alone, looking for friendlies to form up on, or they were more concerned about identifying the correct DZ. For those aircraft flying without navigators or pathfinder equipment, it was a near-impossible task. Looking for landmarks was one way, but if they strayed some miles off course, this was very difficult. In some cases, pilots were flicking the green light on knowing they were approaching the east coast or having attempted to locate the DZ. This caused mis-drops of varying severity.

"Those few minutes in the soup felt like eternity in a blindfold. When we finally broke out of the fog, there were scattered planes left and right and in front of us. I breathed a sigh of relief — but not for long. We had little time to get the plane back down from 1,500 to 700ft for the upcoming drop"
1st Lt Julian Rice, 316th Troop Carrier Group

Flying above the clouds, the situation was worse. If a formation had been maintained by flying above the clouds and good navigation had kept that formation on the correct course, that was a bonus, but the DZ still had to be located. When the cloud ended, the DZ may have been visible a few miles ahead, but you had a formation of C-47s flying more than 2,000ft too high, and needing to descend to the correct altitude while maintaining the right jump speed. Add into the mix aircraft from advanced serials criss-crossing the countryside to find their DZ, and you had chaos.

The pilots had several ways to reduce their air speed in a descent or immediately after descending to the correct height. The first was to destroy what few aerodynamic properties a C-47 has. They could do this by dropping the flaps or 'kicking' the rudder to rock the aircraft. ❯

ABOVE:
Taken prior to September 1944's Arnhem landings, but a scene redolent of earlier operations that year: Brig Gen Anthony C. McAuliffe addresses his CG-4 glider pilots at Aldermaston, with C-47s of the 434th TCG's 72nd TCS also on hand.
NATIONAL ARCHIVES AND RECORDS ADMINISTRATION

This, most likely, contributed to the paratroopers' belief that pilots were attempting to 'fly around' the flak. At less than 1,000ft, and with most of the post-mission flak damage reports by groundcrew attributing that damage to small arms fire, it's debatable and probably unlikely that pilots could avoid the flak. They could only see what was in front of them, and what was in front of them was not going to hit them.

"So, just step on the brakes, right? What brakes? To reduce the speed of a C-47 in a hurry, you get resourceful quick. Co-pilot Wells extended the flaps and lowered the landing gear to help produce drag, while I kicked the rudder and yanked elevator and aileron controls around to slow the descent. The resulting ride down was rough. It may have caused anger among the paratroops"
1st Lt Julian Rice, 316th Troop Carrier Group

The pilots could, if necessary, drop the aircraft's landing gear, which created such drag as to drastically reduce speed in a short space of time. This had its own quite apparent dangers. If trying to reduce speed while descending, the pilots could use another method, which was to kill all throttle and drop the manifold pressure right back to the point where the engine was idling. This caused the propeller to spin in the wind, creating an airbrake effect. However, this generated tremendous noise. The spinning prop made the engine sound as though it was being pushed hard, thus explaining the perception among paratroopers that pilots were increasing air speed just before a drop.

"Only the people flying and operating those aircraft were qualified to comment in detail on such things as air speed, altitude and attitude of the aircraft. Anything else is pure speculation and should be treated as such"
1st Lt William M. Prindible, 316th Troop Carrier Group

Also worth considering is how long it took a group of paratroopers to vacate an aircraft and how far they would travel in that time. A well-trained stick of paratroopers can exit an aircraft in around 12 seconds, at which time it will have travelled between 0.3 and 0.5 miles. It may

seem inconsequential, but this can be the difference between making your DZ following a short walk or being lost for days.

Take, for example, the saga of Lt Col Louis Mendez, commanding officer of the 3rd Battalion, 508th PIR. Mendez was lost for around three days, suggesting he missed his DZ by a considerable distance. In fact, he did so by around two miles, but because his aircraft was slightly off course and the green light was perhaps a little late, he was carried south of the Douve river. Had his stick been released just 20 seconds earlier, he may have landed on the correct side of the Douve and a short walk from his objectives. Similarly, an aircraft-load of men from the 507th PIR was split due to a refusal in the door after half the stick had already vacated. By the time the hesitant jumper had been cleared, the aircraft had travelled around two miles and dropped the remainder of the stick on the eastern side of the Merderet river, between La Fière and Sainte-Mère-Église. While half the men landed roughly within their regimental area, the second half ended up fighting as part of a composite unit at the La Fière bridgehead and were not able to rejoin their own regiment for three days.

In summary, the drops carried out by IX Troop Carrier Command on D-Day were compromised the moment they hit a cloud bank, or 'wall of fog', which had not been mentioned as part of the briefing. It caused the break-up of many of the formations and resulted in pilots having to decide how best to react. We can count on several instances in which pilots made multiple passes over an area to locate the correct DZ. While the mis-drops were unfortunate and often costly, the suggestion that troop carrier failures caused them is unfair. Some time spent analysing the causes and the results indicates that there's much more to it. I believe the myths of erratic behaviour, flying to avoid flak and increased air speeds can be explained. Perhaps it is time to consider not that the pilots were flying in the best interests of self-preservation but more to rectify a situation affected by the unexpectedly poor weather conditions.

In the words of the late Randy Hils, "The letters in my possession are the words of honourable men seeking redress as gentlemen." **A**

66 *The D-Day drops were compromised the moment they hit a cloud bank* 99